Is your cat too fat?

Is your cat too fat?

BRONWEN MEREDITH

WITH ILLUSTRATIONS BY GRAHAM OAKLEY

WEIDENFELD & NICOLSON
LONDON

Contents

Introduction

Cats are now the preferred pets. Their independent ways, their secret love of affection, together with their ability to spend long hours on their own make them ideal pets for the way that we live today. Small spaces and busy lives can easily accommodate the needs of a cat – and they are very nice to come home to.

There are now almost 8 million cats in Britain and a staggering 55 million in the USA, though Indonesia holds the record for the highest number. Quite how these figures are established I'm not quite sure, as not all cats are registered with vets, nor do they all eat commercial foods (a good source for statistics). Then there are countless feral cats, who seem to survive and multiply rather well.

However many cats there are roaming around, it's the house cat that's up against an increasingly endemic problem. Yes, I'm talking about your beloved pet, whom you treat so well. The problem is obesity. Researchers estimate that on average 20 to 25 per cent of cats are overweight, which puts them at high risk for a potential myriad of serious medical problems, not to mention a shorter life. Would you wish that on your cat? It sounds only too human, for we seem to be inflicting on our treasures our own current evolutionary scourge: each generation gets fatter. Why?

Is it the same old story? A question of too much food and too little exercise? Not exactly. First of all, cats don't need that much activity, instead depending on short, high-energy spurts of action to keep fit. Granted, most of us are inclined to overfeed our cats, but it is the quality of food that is at the root of this new fat phenomenon rather than the quantity. We are definitely doing something wrong.

Now, I'm not a veterinarian but I've reared cats for years in the Mediterranean, northern Europe and the USA. I have also written many books on human health and nutrition. Early on I decided to extend to my cats the food philosophy that I followed for myself: fresh, natural foods with the very minimum of processed products. Why should they be forced to eat anything less? They have all led very healthy and contented lives.

Most vets take the view that cats can live perfectly well on commercial foods as long as the necessary nutrients are there – and many do. Sceptics say that this is rather like the white-bread and breakfast-cereal syndrome, whose fortified additives are nowhere near approaching the benefits of the real, wholesome grain. A healthy diet is not necessarily the sum of its chemical components. What is more, there could very well be some vital element in natural foods that is still unknown to the scientist.

Pet nutrition is coming under scrutiny as a result of the concern of the pets' owners. Just as we have become more health conscious about our own diet, and owe a huge debt to such early nutritional mavericks as Adele Davies, so challenging questions regarding the true value of pet food are now coming from the ranks rather than the establishment.

The new protagonist in the realm of pet nutrition is the animal naturopath, who advocates disease prevention and cure through diet, botanicals and the selective use of homeopathic treatments. This enlightened attitude argues that although small amounts of additives in commercial foods may be declared safe, many substances cannot be excreted. These build up over the weeks and months and are stored in inert fat. So not only is it just a matter of time before the cat's health is endangered, but the cat also needs to acquire more fat to store the toxins – another hazard.

If you can get your cat to eat wholesome food containing all the vital elements you will not only have a healthier cat but a thinner one, too. But can the right nutrition also really help the cat's body to overcome various physical ailments? The answer is yes. Amazingly, diet also affects temperament: nervous cats calm down and lazy cats perk up.

Diet is a tool that every cat-owner can use to build up their cat's health and resistance to disease, extend their life and encourage a contented nature. The trend for real food for pets started a few years ago, and owners who then went in for home-cooking certainly got more than their fair share of ridicule. They are now considered role models for those of us who really care about our cats.

Meal times are big events in a cat's life. When we feed our cats it is a prime social occasion when we interact together – and perhaps the one time when we think we are really needed and appreciated. The smell, taste and consistency of food influence a cat's attitude towards eating. I'm sure cats have a discerning palate and a low boredom threshold.

And cats are canny: they instinctively know what's good. Just consider this: a noted animal researcher in a Canadian laboratory set out to prove that hunger and hunting are controlled by quite distinct, though interconnected, parts of the brain, which he found to be true. In doing so he also discovered something very significant about a cat's food preferences. He allowed experienced rat-catching cats to start a meal of commercial cat food and then arranged for live rats to run past the bowls. All the cats immediately stopped eating, caught the rats, dragged them back to the food bowls and calmly carried on eating as if nothing had happened. He concluded that cats hunted for the hell of it, but preferred canned food. However, if the canned food was replaced with fresh salmon, most cats finished the salmon before dealing with the rat. They're no fools those felines!

With that I rest my case.

Your cat can be persuaded to vary his diet. It may mean he will go hungry for a few days while he makes his point, but he won't starve, and will eventually come round.

1 Cats are carnivores

I take it for granted that if you are reading this book you are mad about cats. This means that there's no need for me to carry on about the remarkable benefits of living with a pussycat, so I'll show great restraint by simply saying that cats are the most special of pets and that more and more people are realising it.

However, we are inclined to love our cats to the misguided extent of treating them as human offspring, happy in our pampering and indulgence of what we think are their innermost needs and desires. In doing so we are unconsciously doing them a great disservice, for we frequently overlook a vital and fundamental element of their natures: cats are carnivores, a genetic fact that is at the core of their behaviour, nutritional requirements and consequent health. If we encourage them to go against the natural grain, it is our fault if we end up with a big, fat cat and its resulting, inevitable ailments.

Cats are also canny creatures and know when they're on to a good thing. They are perfectly content to stifle their basic instincts – anything for a cosy, cosseted life! Over thousands of years cats have proved to be the most adaptable of animals, going from the desert to the divan with equal equanimity. Yet, oddly enough, the cat's physiology has changed only slightly. In the interests of being the best of carers you should know a little about it.

THE EGYPTIAN INITIATIVE

It is generally accepted that the domestication of cats started in Egypt in around 4000 BC, when the African wild cat started to share the same habitat as humans. Whether this was humanity's choice or a clever move on the part of the cat is not known, but for the latter it was definitely a life-style change for the better. After spending aeons in the desert, with its hot days and freezing nights – let alone its scarcity of succulent prey – a granary full of mice and equally tasty things must have seemed like heaven.

And the heavenly realm is exactly where cats were believed to live, as gods. From around 1600 BC a powerful cat cult arose, associated with the goddess Bastet, who took the head of a cat and was influential in the realm of fertility, among other female attributes. The cat-worshipping cult lasted for 2,000 years.

However, the lives of those early domesticated cats would appear to have been somewhat ambiguous, for paintings and sculptures depict them not only as sitting on pedestals, but also out in the fields doing their expected and mundane mice-catching jobs. But nowhere are cats portrayed at a banquet, or being fed delicate morsels. It was clearly up to them to organise their own meals, an activity that kept them fit and trim and secured their genetic anatomy and heritage.

Cats were regarded as gods in ancient Egypt.

ENTERPRISING COLONISTS

In the beginning, domestic cats were prized to such a degree that they were not allowed to travel outside Egypt, but eventually Phoenician traders smuggled some into Italy and Greece and from there they gradually spread all over Europe, eventually diligently working their way to the New

World as essential members of the households of the first settlers.

The early Christian Church was suspicious of the cat because of its ancient association with paganism, whilst in the Middle Ages cats even became a symbol of witchcraft. The cat was thus reduced to a secretive, skulking life and a feral existence. Nevertheless, it survived with commendable bravado.

Today's huge feline population and cats' predominance as pets clearly demonstrates their capacity for hanging on in there, as well as their ability to look for ways in which to improve their living standards. Somehow cats eased their way back into popular acceptance and went with great style and verve from the farmyard and the street to the larder and kitchen, and finally back onto the comfortable couch.

Smug with their achievement, they have practically regained their deified status within early Egyptian idolatry. In fact, in some ways they are better off, for we now offer them food as well as shelter. Ideally, we should be providing them with the same nutrients that have kept cats remarkably fit, resourceful and astonishingly procreative for thousands of years. Alas this is not always the case.

BODY BASICS

Cats are mammals, as are humans, so we have many physiological structures and functions in common. The ways in which the cat differs from other mammals – certain skeletal adjustments, specialised muscle responses and a modified digestive system – are, however, directly related to its carnivorous habits. It is interesting to note that these inherited physiological systems have hardly changed since the beginning of the period of the cat's domestication – an unusual evolutionary phenomenon. Clearly the cat was determined to retain its original components and not allow humans to redesign it in their own image.

When we feed and cook for our cat, it is vitally important that we remember that a predominantly flesh-based diet and a distinctive digestive system have served generations of the cat's feline ancestors – both in the wild and as pets – superbly well. Cats possess teeth designed for grabbing, tearing and ripping their prey, short intestines and a large liver. The wrong food will play havoc with the cat's metabolism.

SOME CAT FACTS

The persecution of the cat during the Middle Ages is cited as the primary reason for the lack of variety amongst European breeds and the prevalence of the moggie. Forced to hide away, cats got on with surviving and reproducing. The result is that today's moggies are extremely robust, having been bred from the healthiest and toughest genes. Although the pure breeds receive more publicity, most cats are moggies. They also live longer than pedigree cats.

SOME CAT FACTS

The odour that really turns cats on is catnip. They go on a trip of delight, often rolling around in it with abandoned glee. Why? Because it contains a mild hallucinogenic essential oil which is chemically similar to a substance excreted in her urine by a queen cat. Toms, of course, are the most wildly affected, though neutered cats and queens get a bit of a high too. Catnip is often found in manufactured cat beds, pillows and toys. You can also buy it or grow your own.

It is important that you know that your cat's stomach is quite small: when empty it is approximately 2 cm in diameter. It's the perfect size to accommodate a mouse, whose body mass is equal to two or three tablespoons of food. Nor does the stomach's capacity vary to any significant degree between breeds, as all pet cats are relatively small – underneath the fur and fat – and are more or less uniform in size (unlike dogs, who differ enormously).

SMELL: THE PRIME LIFELINE

Cats have around 19 million nerve endings in the membrane that lines their noses, and all are concerned with smell. Compare that to a mere 5 million in humans and you'll quickly conclude that the cat's olfactory sense is extremely acute.

'High' on catnip. This apparently innocuous plant contains a mild hallucinogenic essential oil, the smell of which is wildly appealing, especially to tom cats.

It is activated by serious sniffing, not through normal breathing. What owner hasn't noticed that their cat loves to hang around the kitchen flexing its nose when food is cooking? It clearly enjoys the aromas and wants you to know it.

Cats are equally sensitive to what is bad, having particularly sharp olfactory antennae that are finely attuned to odours involving nitrogen compounds. These are present in food that is just starting to go off, let alone in food that is decidedly rancid. This is why your cat appears fussy about some food, for it will reject anything that is less than fresh.

In addition, cats boast a rather extraordinary and very well-developed physical mechanism which reacts to both smell and taste. It is called Jacobson's organ and is situated on the roof of the mouth. Not only is it important for recognising acceptable food, but also for keeping track of territorial boundaries.

Jacobson's organ also accounts for that peculiar, trance-like look that can be compared to a half grin and half nose-twitch – one that is displayed by all cats from time to time. Scientists explain this as 'tasting scent' and have given it a German-derived name: flehming. With apparently no exact translation in English, I like to think of it as the feline equivalent of our 'grin and bear it' – in the feline case, 'grin and check it'.

WHAT ABOUT TASTE?

Cats have a sense of taste, but not to any great degree. After all, how tasty can a small rodent be? Cats actually use their tongues more as hands, rather than as flavour-testing organs. The cat's tongue has the most abrasive surface of that of any mammal. The main, central channel of the tongue's top surface is covered with backward-pointing projections – rather like flexible miniature quills – and these are used not only for taking up food and water, but also for grooming.

The tongue's taste buds are limited to the tip, situated along narrow strips on either side and in a cluster at the back. This means that they do not exactly permit direct access to taste sensations, so while we can immediately detect sweet and sour, bitter and salty tastes, cats have a limited, and somewhat vague, reaction. They taste sour best, then bitter, and they recognise salt but show no significant response to sweet tastes. Of course, kittens receive

SOME CAT FACTS

Their sense of smell is very important to cats, who use it to identify foods. However, according to research, food recognition is based on smell, as well as the cat's past experience, rather than on taste. Their memory of food is important because the number of taste buds in a cat's tongue is relatively low. Humans, for example, have 9,000, pigs 15,000, dogs 1,700 and cats a mere 475. A point to note: because cats use their noses to classify types of food, if its nose is blocked as the result of a virus or dirt, your cat will have a poor appetite and may perhaps not eat at all.

SOME CAT FACTS

All the ancient pure breeds, such as Persian, Siamese, Burmese, Abyssinian and Angora, come from non-Christian areas, where cats were treasured and kept closely confined over many generations. In Europe, the concept of breeding cats of pedigree did not develop until the middle of the nineteenth century. The first British national cat show, held at London's Crystal Palace, was in 1871, and was followed six years later by the establishment of the National Cat Club. The first American cat show was held in New York in 1895.

lactose (a form of sugar) in their mother's milk, but cannot always digest such sugars later on in life. In fact, contrary to the traditional image of cats lapping up milk, milk is not a natural food for your carnivorous cat.

THE GOOD PREY GUIDE

Two myths prevail about the cat's food preferences: that it loves birds and fish. In the wild, however, cats are neither keen bird-catchers nor fish-eaters.

The image of a cat licking its lips over fish bones is a cartoon creation, and it is we who were responsible for introducing fish into the cat's diet. Except for a rare Far-Eastern breed, cats don't instinctively catch fish. Most cats hate water, though they may paw and tease a goldfish in a bowl. It's the fishes' movement that appeals to them, not the resultant meal.

As for birds, only a few cats are stirred to kill them. Again, it's the fluttering that challenges them, and your proud cat will bring its victim to you simply to receive an admiring pat on the head rather than to make a serious contribution to the kitchen. On the other hand, if it caught a mouse it would most likely go behind a bush to eat it and you'd be none the wiser. You're thus more aware of the bird as a potential victim and therefore think that that's the main target.

Cats prefer to eat small mammals, mostly rodents. They also like young rabbits and hares, although the mature adults are just too big, not only for cats to catch but also to consume. In warm climates they'll also eat insects and small reptiles.

Pet cats usually eat very little of what they catch, but their method of eating hasn't changed since they became domesticated. Small mammals are eaten from the head down, though if the skull is resistant the meal will start at the neck. Practically every part of the victim is consumed, including the stomach and its recently ingested contents. Consumption follows the direction of the fur pile and the skin is removed by hanging on to it with the teeth and then tugging and shaking. Birds are plucked first, which is a tedious process involving pulling and spitting out the feathers, which must be the main reason why cats will only resort to eating birds if they are desperately hungry.

2 How fit, how fat?

It is generally accepted that a significant proportion of pet cats are overweight. Eating too much and exercising too little are clearly factors in weight gain, but some dietitians also believe that the quality of food often counts more than calories, and this is especially pertinent in view of the cat's small body, limited stomach capacity and inability to metabolise many toxins.

WHAT MAKES CATS FAT?

Undesirable weight gain is not just due to excessive food intake and a lack of exercise, though both play an important part. Equally responsible for causing feline obesity are the following factors: deficient nutrients, toxic food additives, and the cat's physical and mental states. Consider this list of potential causes of obesity.

Calories: these do add up, of course, and if your cat keeps stuffing itself its excess energy intake will be stored as fat and it will simply get fatter and fatter. Apparently there seems to be no limit to how fat a cat can get. For every 3,000–3,500 of excess calories ingested, your cat will put on about ½ kg (1 lb) of fat, which could be an increase of 20 per cent of its body weight.

Junk food: this is an extremely significant cause of weight gain, because the additives and preservatives contained in many commercial foods encourage fatty deposits. Research has shown that overweight cats are more likely to have been fed dry foods, either as part, or all, of their diet.

Snacks: these make a big contribution to obesity, so cut them out (unless they are of the healthy variety, as described in the recipe section). Generously dispensing snacks may make you feel good, but you are certainly not doing your cat any favours.

Neutering: although neutering is very beneficial in many ways, it seems to affect the cat's ability to control its appetite, which in the

SOME FAT FACTS

A cat's weight does not represent a direct link between the intake of calories and energy output. It has been suggested that the cat's metabolic rate is affected by both seasonal and daily rhythms. Food intake is at its highest in the autumn and at its lowest in the spring, while weight is at its lowest in the summer and peaks in mid-winter.

The concept of feeding a uniform product as opposed to a diet with no variety or fresh food is contrary to all current human medical thinking.

British naturopathic veterinarian SCOTT SNELLGROVE.

natural state is otherwise very well regulated. Males put on more weight than females.

Exercise: house-bound cats are, of course, at a big disadvantage when it comes to opportunities to take exercise, and have to be encouraged to dash around and climb things. Unlike dogs, however, they don't actually need to engage in too much activity.

Boredom: if you don't give your cat things to play with, or dedicate a certain amount of your undivided attention to it from time to time, it is just going to resign itself to coping with boredom by curling up in a ball and sleeping for hours on end. That's bad news for its mental and physical health, and you are being the selfish one. Get going and become an entertainer!

Rearing: the development of feline fat cells, although partly genetically influenced, is largely established during the period of early growth: from birth up to six months. Once formed, the fat cells are there for life, and because dieting only reduces the size of the cells (not the number), they only too easily swell up again. Overweight kittens make fat adult cats, so take care of your cat from the start.

Age: like us, cats slow down as they get older and consequently require less food. However, older cats are not necessarily the fatties. Most overweight cats are middle-aged, that is, between four and ten years old.

TOXINS CAUSE FAT

In the world of complementary medicine, fat is considered to be a toxin storehouse. The argument is that the chemicals and additives contained in processed foods, which cannot be dissolved in water and excreted through the kidneys, are dissolved in fat.

A British veterinarian, Scott Snellgrove, confirms the theory that toxins tend to accumulate in fat, thus keeping them away from the rest of the body in a protective response, but adds that it is not absolutely scientifically certain that fat is laid down as a response to the toxins themselves.

Cats are also at a disadvantage when it comes to coping with

Boredom is one of the main reasons why your cat sleeps for hours. Become an entertainer and encourage it to get moving...

food additives and preservatives, as they are unable to detoxify these fast or efficiently to excrete these poisonous substances.

If you allow your cat to get and stay fat you are putting it at the forefront of a firing line of a potentially long list of physical disorders. Obesity is the prime cause of diabetes, and also of a common, and potentially fatal, liver disease called hepatic lipidosis. Fat cats are more prone to high blood pressure, which contributes to heart and lung problems. Arthritis is a further threat, along with nerve malfunction and reproductive limitations. Life expectancy is greatly reduced by obesity, for the kidneys' action slows down, and cancer becomes increasingly prevalent. In other words, your poor, obese cat may fall victim to more or less any disease or bodily malfunction as a result of its weight.

How to tell if your cat is fat

If your cat is really fat you'd have to be blind not to notice it. But it is surprising how many cat-owners have a blind spot when it comes to their beloved pet and who therefore fail to recognise either the development of its increased girth or the extent of its obesity.

The ideal cat, from the health point of view, is well proportioned and agile. When viewed from above, a waist should be easily defined beneath the ribs. The ribs themselves should be covered with only a minimal amount of fat, and the same applies to the back and neck area, while the abdomen should be firmly tucked up.

The obese cat, on the other hand, has heavy deposits of fat over its back, neck, ribcage and sometimes even on its legs. Its face can become jowled, as in a plump human, but the most overweight area is the abdomen, which is covered with extensive amounts of fat, making it rounded and notably pendulous, so that it nearly touches the ground.

A cat's weight gain can creep up on you unawares. Cats have an inexplicable tendency to look in perfectly good condition on one day and sloppily fat the next. An early sign is a lack of interest in grooming, so that its coat begins to look unkempt and straggly, resulting in something of a vagabond look. (Washing involves quite a bit of effort, and to keep up a spruce appearance the routine should be repeated an exhausting fifteen to thirty times a day. What fat cat is going to keep that up?) Excess fat can also hinder the cat's access to many parts of its body, thus limiting its usual ability to

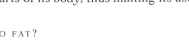

perform contortionist manoeuvres. So don't be caught offguard: catch the fat before it really takes hold by making regular fat-assessment tests.

THE WEIGH-IN

An obvious first step is to find out the exact weight of your cat, yet few owners do so. It is very important to see how the figure compares to the average for its type (see the 'Weight-watching' chart). Don't even attempt to put the cat on any sort of scales – it's a frustrating and invariably useless exercise, not to mention a battle of the wills. The most practical way is for you to stand on the scales while holding the cat, then to weigh yourself alone; an easy subtraction provides the required figure.

Your cat will quickly realise the implications of stepping onto the bathroom scales, and will resist your efforts strongly.

Weight-watching

Cats are generally similar in size, with only a few, special breeds being either extremely light- or heavyweight. The considered ideal weight for the average moggie and pure-bred cat is between 3.5 and 5.8 kilograms (8 to 12½ lbs). If your cat registers an additional 15 per cent or more, it is definitely fat; the undesirable weigh-in figures range from approximately 4.5 to 7.7 kilograms (10 to 17 lbs) and upwards.

It is, however, difficult to state the exact optimal weights for cats, particularly those that have been randomly bred. Feline types vary from place to place, though in general the stockier, sturdier cats are found in cold countries, and the lighter, leaner cats live in warmer climates and the tropics. That, of course, is the natural order of things but, as pets, today all kinds of cats are found everywhere.

Weight is not a precise indicator of fat levels, but the figures given below are a good guide as to the healthy limits.

BREED	WEIGHT IN KILOGRAMS	WEIGHT IN POUNDS
Average Moggie	3.5–6 kg	8–13 lb
Abyssinian	4.5–8 kg	10–17 lb
American Bobtail	3.5–7.5 kg	8–16 lb
American Shorthair	4–7.5 kg	9–16 lb
American Wirehair	4–7.5 kg	9–16 lb
Angora	2.5–5.5 kg	6–12 lb
Balinese	3–5.5 kg	7–12 lb
Bengalese	5–9.5 kg	11–21 lb
Burmese	4–7 kg	9–15 lb
Bombay	3–5.5 kg	7–12 lb
British Shorthair	3.5–8 kg	8–18 lb
Chartreux	3.5–8 kg	8–18 lb
Cornish Rex	2.5–5 kg	5–11 lb

Cymric	.4–6 kg	.9–13 lb
Devon Rex	.2.5–4.5 kg	.6–10 lb
Egyptian Mau	.2.25–5 kg	.5–11 lb
European Shorthair	.3.5–7.5 kg	.8–16 lb
Havana Brown	.2.5–5 kg	.6–11 lb
Japanese Bobtail(Long & Shorthair)	.2.5–4.5 kg	.6–10 lb
Korat	.2.5–5.5 kg	.6–12 lb
Maine Coon	.4.5–10 kg	.10–22 lb
Manx	.3.5–6 kg	.8–13 lb
Nebelung	.2.5–5 kg	.6–11 lb
Norwegian Forest Cat	.3.5–9.5 kg	.8–21 lb
Ocicat	.2.5–7 kg	.6–15 lb
Oriental Longhair	.4–6.5 kg	.9–14 lb
Oriental Shorthair	.4–6.5 kg	.9–14 lb
Persian	.4–7.5 kg	.9–16 lb
Ragdoll.	.4.5–9.5 kg	.10–21 lb
Russian Shorthair	.3–6 kg	.8–13 lb
Scottish Fold (Long & Shorthair)	.2.5–6 kg	.6–13 lb
Selkirk Rex	.3–5.5 kg	.7–12 lb
Siamese	.2.5–5.5 kg	.6–12 lb
Siberian Forest Cat	.4.5–9.5 kg	.10–21 lb
Singapura	.2–4 kg	.4–9 lb
Somali	.3.5–5.5 kg	.8–12 lb
Sphynx	.3.5–7.5 kg	.8–16 lb
Tonkinese	.2.5–6 kg	.6–13 lb
Turkish Angora	.2.5–5.5 kg	.6–12 lb
Turkish Van	.3.5–8.5 kg	.8–19 lb

Source: Dr Paolo Assogna, Rome.

THE PINCH TEST

The pinch test is a good human method of measuring obesity: just grab a piece of skin and see how much it pulls away from the skeletal and muscular frame. When pinch-testing a cat, however, there is a subtle difference.

As the cat has a lot of loose skin, particularly around the neck, and the really taut skin is on the legs, you have to feel for the fat rather than measure the pinch of skin in centimetres. This is not as difficult as it sounds, and you will quickly acquire a professional thumb of judgment. Of course, your cat will not be too happy about it, so you will have to sneak in the odd feel every now and then, rather than dealing with the whole body in one examination.

There should be just a light cover of fat under the skin: for example, you should be able to feel the ribs, although you will not see them. This is the primary area to check. Others include the back, neck and abdomen (though weight gain on the abdomen is invariably obvious, and any pinching here is apt to make cats particularly irritated).

A Cornell University veterinarian research team set these six basic shapes as a guide for owners to assess the physical contours of their cats. The ideals are optimal-lean (3) and optimal (4).

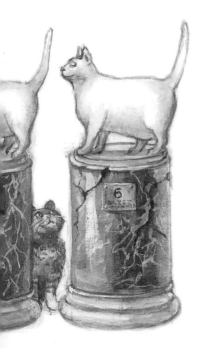

THE SHAPE ASSESSMENT

The standard physical contours of cats, both standing and lying, are useful guidelines when estimating the distribution and quantity of feline fat. Compare your cat's contours with the series of six feline shapes which were used by a Cornell University veterinarian research team to help cat-owners estimate their cats' fat situation at a glance.

The body outlines are identified: cachectic (weak), lean, optimal-lean, optimal, heavy and obese. If you have a long-haired cat, try to envisage the shape underneath its pelt, though the fur usually follows the skin in an even pattern so the silhouette remains a pretty accurate indicator. The optimal-lean and optimal shapes are clearly the best.

An interesting result of the Cornell University survey was the curious fact that owners were clearly tougher when judging their cats' shape than the more objective vets. The researchers estimated 58 per cent of cats to be in the acceptable range covered by the optimal-lean or optimal categories, whereas the owners only allowed for 47 per cent.

WEIGHT-LOSS PROGRAMMES

When you put your cat on a diet, you basically follow the same rules as you would apply to yourself. The problem is that you can't explain the whys and wherefores to your cat, and it will be most indignant about any sudden change in its eating habits, blaming you entirely and letting you know it.

We are all cowards when it comes to upsetting our cats, being loath to take on a hard-hearted role and also being fearful of losing our pet's affection. How can you get it across to your cat that you are taking these decisive dieting steps for its own good? Only through deception, that is, by letting your cat think that it's in control of the choices.

The first aim is to get your cat to agree to switch from a predominantly processed-food diet to a mostly natural one. The second is surreptitiously to serve smaller portions without your cat realising it. If you achieve both, your cat will slowly and unwittingly shed its flab, and be healthier and happier for it.

First check out the nutritious-food facts in the chapter titled 'Getting the diet right'. If your cat has been fed processed food, particularly if it's been eating the same brand for ages, you will probably encounter a high degree of stubbornness if you attempt to make a drastic change in its diet. You should start by mixing fresh food with its habitual diet, and gradually increase the ratio over a period of weeks until your cat is eventually primarily fed on home-made fare.

Even with the easy-does-it method, some cats will go on strike and will not eat the new combination, thereby hoping to make you change your mind and go back to serving the usual nosh. Don't give in. Leave the food around for no more than half an hour, then take it away and try again a few hours later. In this way your cat is making the choice whether to eat or not. If it wants to starve, that's its decision. Just keep on offering – it will make you feel less guilty anyway. An important note: always prepare a new mix of food each time, as cats will not touch anything that's not comletely fresh, let alone second-hand.

Don't panic if it looks as though your cat would rather starve to death than eat anything but product X: its instinct for survival is strong and it will finally come around. In any case, a short fast aids inner cleansing, and a cat can furthermore go for many days without eating. Just make sure that water is available.

Cut down on quantity

It is obvious that your fat cat also has to eat less if it is to lose weight. At the same time as you are making a gradual change toward a more healthy diet, you should also reduce the portions of food, but so slightly that your cat won't notice. This strategy is not purely designed to safeguard the cat's peace of mind. If a dietary change is too drastic, it will result in a rapid release of fat into the bloodstream which, if heavily toxic, can cause serious problems, including the potentially fatal liver disease hepatic lipidosis.

Aim to reduce the portions that you serve your cat to the equivalent of two good tablespoons of food per day (though note that this is an average estimate). You alone can sensibly judge the correct quantities, since they depend on both the size of your cat and the amounts of food that is accustomed to. It is important to remember that although your cat won't be eating as much food, it will certainly be enjoying healthier, more satisfying, nutrients.

SOME FAT FACTS

Cats appear to be quite content to eat smaller meals, as long as there are enough of them. The British animal researcher John Bradshaw says in his book *The behaviour of the domestic cat:*

> If palatable food is available all the time in a form that does not 'stale', cats will take small meals (typically 12–20) throughout both the day and night. The way that meal size and the interval between meals is determined is not fully understood, but over the course of a few hours the majority of cats are able to regulate their calorie intakes to match their requirements, usually by decreasing the content of each meal rather than by reducing the number of meals.

If your cat resists a new mix of food, you must persevere. It will come around eventually.

SOME FAT FACTS

A cat's individual food needs are so variable that when you first change the quantity and quality of meals you have to be extremely observant and ready to readjust them on a daily basis, according to both your cat's bodily and behavioural responses. Your cat should never lose weight too quickly.

LESS FOOD BUT MORE MEALS

Serving smaller meals more often has proved a most successful slimming plan for cats, but it is not always practical as you may have to be absent from home for long periods.

High-quality protein and fats, however, will satisfy your cat, even when presented in skimpy portions. The Canadian veterinarian and author Edmund R Dorosz suggests feeding the cat a mere teaspoon of nutritious food every three or four hours. The small portions will allow the stomach to shrink so that hunger is easily satisfied, and the combination of protein and fat will givethe cat a feeling of fullness – it also tastes good. He suggests

the following ingredients: roast chicken, turkey, duck, beef or lamb, ground, good-quality beef, liver, kidney, fish, kippers, sardines, cooked egg, cottage cheese and yogurt.

SLIMMING RULES

Prevention is best: train kittens to eat well

As has already been mentioned, fat cells are mostly formed during the first six months of a cat's life (although genetics also play a part in this). A fat kitten becomes a fat adult, and overfeeding your cat when it is young is thus the worst thing you can do.

A kitten should gain about 1 to 2 grams a day per kilogram of the estimated adult weight for the breed. Nutritional quality at this stage is vital. If kittens are given food which contains more calories than protein it can result in disproportionate growth. Fat accumulated when young also puts undue stress on a kitten's soft, growing bones and joints. If anything, it is better slightly to underfeed your cat at this stage in its life.

The noted naturalist and author Juliette de Baïracli Levy gives very sound advice in *The complete herbal handbook for the dog and cat*, suggesting that a wide variety of fresh foods be introduced into the kitten's diet at six weeks – or even earlier if the kitten seems to need it. She gives her kittens milk (other than their mother's) at three weeks, and at four weeks weans them on a gruel mixture which can be purchased in health-food shops: for each kitten make a paste from one teaspoon of gruel and one teaspoon of honey; stir in one teaspoon of warm water, then add two dessertspoons of warm milk. She prefers to use raw milk, which is not always available. If your kittens have trouble digesting cow's milk, try goat's.

This formula is given to the kittens at breakfast and supper time, while at noon and again in the mid-afternoon the kittens get flaked barley in milk. At six weeks, the mid-afternoon and evening meals are replaced with several teaspoons of cooked fish or raw meat, both finely chopped (not minced), with the addition of a pinch of powdered kelp and also half a teaspoon of finely cut salad and perhaps leaf greens.

Between five and six weeks of age kittens have a full set of sharp teeth and can tackle most things, but still have to be gradually introduced to a varied adult diet. The suggested feeding schedule from this time until they are four months old is as follows:

The slimming rules: be kind but firm when explaining the new programme to your cat. This list could be pinned to the wall beside its basket as a salutary reminder to both of you.

Slimming rules

- be determined and set a weight goal
- regularly check weight loss and body condition
- feed less but more often
- gradually reduce daily intake by approximately one-third
- use high-quality natural ingredients
- be vigilant about the correct protein/fat/carbohydrate balance
- protect health with a daily vitamin/mineral supplement
- cut out sweet commercial snacks
- increase exercise and play
- give love and attention
- watch out for behavioural changes
- keep the house temperature reasonably low
- stay firm and don't give in

8 am: gruel with milk and flaked cereals
12 am: milk with a variety of flaked cereals, including barley, maize, rye and oats (but not wheat); add a few drops of oil – sesame, corn or sunflower (not olive); beaten egg yolk can be given on some days, as well as cottage cheese and mozzarella
4 pm: a flesh meal of rabbit, poultry or fish, lightly cooked and shredded; or the best beef or lamb, raw and shredded; add a teaspoon of raw bran and a teaspoon of finely minced raw greens
8 pm: a repeat of the 4 pm meal

Juliette de Baïracli Levy points out that it is impossible to advise on exact quantities because of many variant factors, including exercise, temperament, breed and climate. It is important to watch the kitten's stomach – if it distends after meals, then cut down the amount of food you give it.

WHAT ABOUT OLDER CATS?

You can consider your cat as being old when it is around ten to fourteen years, and even fat cats tend to loose weight naturally in their later years. Although it is decidedly less active, the digestive system usually remains in good order, but there's often a decrease in the acuteness of the cat's senses of smell and taste, which affects its appetite.

Although older cats don't need so many calories, they do require powerful nutrients, particularly vitamins and minerals. A daily supplement of these is therefore a good idea at this stage in a cat's life (see pages 85–87). Food, however, is one of the few pleasures that are left in old age, so if you really care for your cat you should feed it smaller meals more often, and thereby spread the pleasure throughout the day. This feeding method also encourages your cat to trim its weight in the least stressful of ways.

Being more sedentary, the mature cat will not need as much food as when it was in its prime, but remember that food is one of its few remaining pleasures in life.

SOME FAT FACTS

What about the commercial diet foods? These are low in calories and high in indigestible fibre; the fat content is also reduced. The idea is that the bulk will satisfy your pet and that your cat will therefore feel full. But full of what? These so-called 'formulated' diets are of questionable value, and fail to address the real issues of why fat was accumulated in the first place, nor do they have any effect on the cat's appetite control. Indeed, they can be regarded as the feline equivalent of formulated liquid diets for humans.

3 Holistic health for cats

There's a powerful new wave of thought gaining ground within the field of animal care these days. Encouraged by the acceptance and success of alternative therapies for humans, an increasing number of pet-owners and professionals are turning to natural remedies in order to help prevent and cure disease in animals. Surprised? You shouldn't be: surely that old maxim 'nature knows best' is even more applicable to the animal world, in which instinct is all, and this instinct has served furred and feathered creatures admirably for countless generations.

After having studied along established orthodox lines, a select group of veterinarians has chosen to look further afield. They have added qualifications in homeopathy, herbal medicine, acupuncture, chiropractic, oriental and botanical treatments to their official degrees. In other words, they are putting to use and giving new credence to old and traditional beliefs and practices in medical science. And it is working – well. A fundamental tenet of such holistic-health strategies is a firm belief in natural nutrition and the need to educate owners in the intrinsic role that it plays in the overall health of their pets, as well as in weight control where this is particularly significant.

'What animals eat and drink determines health and weight above all else', emphasises Christopher Day, a naturopathic vet from Oxfordshire, England.

There's no substitute for natural food when it comes to body maintenance and the prevention of many disorders. However, fresh is not always good enough. You have to look for the source and also question the feed of animal protein. Fish from polluted waters can be harmful; poultry and meat not naturally fed can contain toxins and dangerous bacteria. The only truly safe food is organic, which can confidently be given raw. This is the optimum diet.

'Another important issue is that if your cat eats the same food day in and day out, no matter how marginal the deficiencies and excesses, these will build up and finally cause problems. Also, the minutest amount of toxic matter, which is invariably tucked out of harm's way in fatty deposits if not quickly eliminated, can accumulate to undesirable levels if ingested on a daily basis.

THE NATUROPATHIC APPROACH

For me, it is not just its nutritional approach that appeals, but the entire naturopathic attitude. As in human holistic practice, the naturopathic vet will look at all aspects of your cat's life in order to establish the cause of a weight problem – though it's you, of course, who has to do all the talking and provide the answers. It is your care that is being judged, and it might not be a pleasant experience. However, you'll be amazed at how much you'll learn about your cat during the holistic vet's initial session, and you will gain a greater understanding of your cat's behaviour and personality, as well as its attitudes and needs.

This in-depth probe into your cat's psyche, as well as your role in its lifestyle, are vital keys to its eating habits and consequent weight and health. Richard H Pitcairn – the pioneer of naturopathic animal care in the USA – puts great emphasis on the empathy between the pet and its owner. He states that to discover how to relate fully to an animal and to feel real care and concern for its welfare and continual physical and psychological well-being is similar to building a close human relationship.

Which pet-owner would refute that? You might receive further, individual insight from your holistic vet. Your relationship with your cat is also a two-sided issue: getting your cat slimmer and healthier, for example, could teach you a thing or two – should you need it (many chubby cats often have chubby owners).

Naturopathic vets take their time. You are not rushed in and out, as usually happens in the standard veterinary clinic, to be sent away with a prescription or two. As Richard Allport, a naturopathic vet from Hertfordshire, England, points out:

> The initial visit is the most important. We have to assess both pet and owner. A lot has to be established. It is not just a matter of examining the cat in front of you – that is routine. More important is to assess things not seen, and only the owner can provide that. I usually need a minimum of an hour for this. Once a comprehensive life-medical picture has been drawn up, we can

You will often
notice that a
special empathy
exists between a
pet and its owner.

then proceed in many directions. Owners are often worried about cost because of the time involved. The first visit may be more than at the usual veterinary clinic – but then those consultations rarely last more than ten minutes. However, natural remedies tend to be less expensive, and we give very comprehensive nutritional advice. We also find fewer follow-ups are necessary.

Another point to consider is that in the alternative veterinarian medical field restrictions on practice are far more stringent than those for humans. Only qualified veterinary surgeons, or practitioners working under their supervision, may treat animals. There is no chance of a charlatan setting up shop – as can sadly sometimes be the case for us.

To find a holistic vet practising in your area, you should check the lists available from two organisations in Britain and the USA. In Britain, there's the British Association of Homeopathic Veterinary Surgeons (Alternative Veterinary Medicine Centre, Chinham House, Stanford-in-the-Vale, Farringdon, Oxon SN7 8NQ), and in the USA there's the American Holistic Veterinary Medical Association (2214 Old Emmorton Road, Bel Air, Maryland 21015). The numbers of the members of both societies are increasing rapidly as more and more owners seek out sympathetic, natural animal care.

THE NUMBER-ONE PRIORITY: GOOD FOOD

Feeding your pet good food seems only too obvious, yet the importance of this is often lightly dismissed by the typical vet, who may endorse the 'complete' concept of commercial products. 'Today it is the holistic vet who's discovering the true role of nutrition in disease prevention and cure through experience and hands-on care. The [veterinary] school curriculum is way behind the times', says New York holistic animal consultant, Anitra Frazier.

This general lack of knowledge regarding nutrition is evident elsewhere, too: you only have to leaf through the majority of currently available cat books to realise that among the many pages devoted to breeds, history, anatomy and general care there are only a few on food. Even these only point out the respective merits of canned, dried and semi-moist commercial offerings, implying that fresh foods are not necessary, and that it is furthermore difficult to feed your cat a balanced diet at home.

Scott Snellgrove, a British vet from St Alban's, England, takes a different view, however.

> It is easy enough to create an overall balanced diet using fresh, varied foods in the appropriate proportions and using common sense. However, it is technically difficult, unnecessary and generally undesirable to try to synthesise the simple 'wonder' product.
>
> 'Manufacturers frequently boast how highly digestible and nutritional their 'complete' products are . . . This may, however, encourage obesity, especially when concentrated, dehydrated foods like biscuits are rapidly consumed with minimal effort.

Anitra Frazier points out that commercial products contain too much fat and salt: 'Even when you see "light" on a product, although this means less fat, it invariably means more salt to make it palatable – and that makes cats gain weight'.

However, it is not necessarily the fat contained within food that puts on the pounds. And some fat is moreover actually good for your cat. 'One of the great problems of many processed foods is the lack of adequate fatty acids like the omega 3 and 6 series, which are vital to cell function', says Scott Snellgrove, adding that some commercial diets now make a big feature of this recent addition to their products. 'Presumably the original "complete" diets were deficient. Unfortunately they often still contain too little, or it is oxidised during processing and storage, making it harmful, not helpful,' he goes on to say.

All holistic vets give a thumbs-down to the majority of processed foods. Nancy Scanlon, an American vet from Sherman Oaks, California, goes further:

> Manufacturers are doing their best to make cats unhealthy and fat. Excess weight is the most obvious result of this unnutritious diet, but also it causes serious diseases. We are seeing more and more cats with diabetes, liver and kidney problems, skin complaints and cancer. It is vital we get the message across to owners that a switch to natural food is the best thing you can do

for your cat. I don't go as far as recommending raw food, because I am very nervous about the increasing percentage of salmonella and e-coli bacteria. A mixture of food, lightly cooked, is the answer. Avoid sticking to one protein source, as cats can literally get addicted to one particular food.

'Standards for commercial pet foods are abysmal – some manufacturers get away with murder', says American vet Jean Hofve, from Denver, Colorado.

The prime thing is to get your cat on a healthy, wholesome diet. Most of the processed foods can't be digested in a useful way for they are all overcooked. I must admit I am not always emphatic about the need for all food to be home-made. We have to be realistic and accept that this would put many owners off. There are some wholesome foods to be found in specialist and health shops, and these can be used to supplement the higher proportion of fresh.

Reading the labels on commercial foods is not of that much help either, as Anitra Frazier points out.

Yes, there are rules that nutrients have to be listed, and yes they are there. But in what form? What are the sources? The lab or the land? Also, bear in mind that canned and dried food are overcooked which can change molecular structure and negate much nutrient value.

Some naturopathic vets go to the other extreme and advocate raw food. William Pollak, an American vet from Fairfield, Iowa, is well known for offering nutritional information (which he also provides on the Internet). 'Freshness is everything, and I strongly believe in the value of raw nutrients. I also advocate a complete switch from one day to the next. You must give your cat the cold-turkey treatment – no pun intended', he says firmly.

Cats can adjust within two to three weeks. And they won't allow themselves to starve, gradually adapting to the new regimen. The adjustment of the owner's attitude is more significant – and often more difficult. Just like humans looked for new resources to cope with their own health problems, we now have to bring alternative medicine to pets, beginning with a radical change in nutrition, then using homeopathic, herbal and oriental therapies for cures that are more in line with nature.

FAT CATS ARE ACTUALLY STARVING

Today's house-bound cat eats far more than its wild or domestic ancestor. We have become over-indulgent, yet also careless, feeders. We are responsible for reducing the cat's signal system that controls appetite and satiety, and possess the misguided notion that a full cat is a contented one, a healthy one. Quite the contrary: 'The more cats eat, the more they starve', claims William Pollak. 'They are overfed and undernourished, and [are] carrying around a lot of toxic matter.'

Anitra Frazier explains the phenomenon of feline big-eaters as being caused by cats' instinctive search for what they really need.

> Cats are constantly reaching out for the missing nutrients. They crave the essentials which they're not getting in processed foods. The result is that they hopefully consume more with no benefit whatsoever, but add the burden of increased weight and toxins.

'Cats will go on demanding food when they are not satisfied with the quality', comments Jean Hofve. 'They do need those essential fatty acids for optimum metabolism – and the taste satisfies too.'

Nancy Scanlon criticises those owners who want their cats to eat the same quantity of food all the time.

> This is unrealistic, and undermines the cat's metabolism, which thrives on, and gains momentum from, change. Nature has its ups and downs. You don't find a fat mouse every day, nor every season. If you prepare meals yourself, you can vary quantity whilst providing optimum protein, fat and fibre.

GETTING THE WEIGHT DOWN

Naturopathic veterinarians are unanimous in their view that a fat cat's weight has to be trimmed gradually and by means of a natural diet. There is general condemnation of the so-called 'diet plans'

offered by manufacturers. As Scott Snellgrove puts it:

> In the event that obesity is caused by product A, product B is
> then recommended – usually a high-fibre, low-calorie version.
> Despite promoting and marketing these diets for many years,
> pet-food manufacturers now acknowledge that neither soluble
> nor insoluble fibre reduces appetite, and that it is of limited
> benefit in weight-loss diets. They fail to address the real problem
> in eating habits.

Don't leave food around . . . the temptation to snack will be too much for even the most self-disciplined cat.

In fact, even the word 'diet' is an anathema when used in the context of reducing the amount of food that a cat is fed. Jean Hofve explains why:

Frankly, I never think of putting cats on a diet as such. I simply change eating habits, meaning the type of food, and they automatically get slimmer over a period of time. I don't get drawn into quantity control unless a cat is really overweight. It also depends on age. Some cats need a little weight, particularly in old age. However, you can get that covering to a healthy level and composition by changing to fresh, natural foods. Unfortunately some cats get so far down the line of toxicity they are too far gone to even attempt to reduce the fat and already have irreversible liver failure. The fattest cat I've ever seen was 26 lbs and probably still is since the owner refused to even consider my advice though he could have been trimmed down gradually. Drastic measures are not good for cats.

'Taking weight off a cat must be done gradually', confirms veterinarian Nancy Scanlon.

Changing to a natural diet is the first step, then introducing more meals of concentrated nutritional value but smaller quantities. In this way cats are immediately satisfied by food content and don't seem concerned about the reduced amount in the bowl. A few hours later, an equally similar nutritious dish will make cats happy, even though the portion is small. Less food of prime nutrients takes off the weight, pleases cats and makes them healthier.

Anitra Frazier couldn't agree more.

In obesity, don't ever think of reducing the amount of a cat's regular food; think of changing the diet and increasing the nutrients. In almost every case, the cat will be satisfied with less. However, don't go too fast, otherwise toxins move into the bloodstream at an alarming rate as fats melt away and can cause fatalities. I am very picky about comfort and safety. An owner must take into account the cat's reaction and feelings to this, the most important aspect of its house-bound life – food and the human interaction. I am never concerned about the rate of weight loss so long as the cat is headed in the right direction.

> The preparation of a cat's daily diet from its individual ingredients provides a sense of achievement and fun. It also brings satisfaction, in that one is taking proper responsibility for the feeding of a feline companion, rather than handing that responsibility over to a commercial body. With modern pressures, this ideal may not be attainable in every family, but any steps taken towards this goal will be of health benefit [to the cat].
>
> British vet CHRISTOPHER DAY.

Why push it? If the cat is getting healthier as well as slimmer, it doesn't need the stressful limits of a time-clock.

She adds one major note of caution, however:

Don't leave food around, no matter what is said about free-feeding. The olfactory antennae of the cat are awesome. It can smell things a mile off, let alone in the kitchen. Think of dried food as cookies and keep [them] in an airtight container. Shut everything away. A cat should not have temptation at the end of its nose all the time. Feed good food at convenient intervals and then remove the bowl.

Cats don't need to have continual access to food. They are carnivores who have been bred to feed spasmodically, and are quite different in mentality, metabolism and functioning from the animal-grazers, to whom grass and foliage are constantly available. It's feast or famine, and you should mimic that pattern when endeavouring to reduce your cat's weight, whether it is on a two- or three-meal routine per day, or more.

Although cats can do without food for quite a while, don't think of putting your cat on an extended fast in the hope of achieving speedy results. 'It is dangerous to fast a cat', says veterinarian Scott Snellgrove. 'An owner may have the best intentions, but sudden and drastic fasting can release fat into the bloodstream, producing fatal hepatic lipidosis.'

A final comment on the toxins that are introduced into your cat's body through processed foods: toxins are cited as being a main contributor to fat accumulation. William Pollak offers the following advice to cat-owners:

The secret to achieving ideal weight and optimum health is detoxification. Excess fat and a cat's contaminated system can be turned around through natural foods, primarily raw. A cat can be sleek within a few months, and within a year I have witnessed the elimination of all disease through diet. Toxins can be slowly withdrawn from the body. Elimination is all. The cat's body is then free and clear to make maximum use of all the good nutrients, those intended and essential elements from nature.

CASE STUDIES

1: Fritzi

Fritzi is a ten-year-old, neutered moggie, adopted originally from the RCSPA in Montreal and later taken to a New York City apartment by his writer-owner. In Montreal he had access to a garden, and although fed canned food was lithe and healthy – due, no doubt, to a bit of outdoor roaming and the odd mouse or two. He did put on a little weight in the winter months, when below-zero temperatures and deep snow kept him indoors.

However, in New York he became a true apartment cat, with not even a terrace, balcony or fire escape to explore. At first he was clearly restless, then he appeared to settle happily into a comfortable, sedentary life – after all, he was by now middle-aged. Canned food remained his staple diet, supplemented by dried, readily available, nibbles. His owner didn't notice that he was getting bigger until she took him to the vet for routine vaccinations.

Much to her amazement, he had almost doubled his weight in eighteen months. The vet didn't seem too concerned, but suggested cutting down on the quantity of food that she fed him. Fritzi didn't take too kindly to this: he became a pest, almost begging for food all the time. Now aware of his size, his owner stood firm and put up with his behaviour, which got steadily worse. What is more, Fritzi did not lose any weight and was certainly more lethargic. Not wanting to incur the expense of another visit to the vet, his owner further reduced the portions of the two meals that she fed him a day, and cut out the dried food.

Only when a health-food-conscious friend pointed out how unkempt Fritzi had become, and expressed horror at hearing about his diet, did the owner even think of giving him natural foods. She couldn't believe that it had never occurred to her.

Full of remorse, she went in search of information on cat nutrition, only to find it limited. Finally, a book on natural care for dogs and cats provided the basic elements with which she could

carry out her new resolve. The plan was this: no more free access to nibbles, only a tablespoon of dried food a day, taken under her supervision; in place of the customary morning and evening meals, food would be served three times a day and at the same time as her own. Meals would comprise a generous tablespoon of chicken, meat or fresh liver, with small amounts of finely chopped and lightly cooked vegetables.

Fritzi was both indignant and apprehensive at first, but after two weeks he was eagerly eating. Within three months the difference in Fritzi was amazing. The most significant improvement was the look and condition of his coat, and he had also regained his former liveliness. As for the weight, that went down from 18 to 10 lbs, but it did take a year.

Fritzi, a New York apartment cat, became a pest, constantly begging for food.

2: Lennox

Lennox was a stray, found wandering in a London garden square. Shorthaired, with beautiful, caramel colouring, he had the look of good breeding and had clearly been well taken care of. Since he was obviously lost, the finder took him to the vet, who said that he was about six months old. Loath to abandon him, the woman who had found him took him home. It was an impulsive move, and not a wise one, as her flat only had an outside window ledge that was more like a plank than a balcony. She also had to travel a lot for her work.

She fed him fresh food twice a day from the start, and left dried food in his bowl when she was out. Lennox seemed happy and thrived; he grew in size, although he didn't become plump. He was very active, as young cats usually are, but his owner made an effort to play with him each day and left toys and balls around the house. She did not have him neutered. When he was a year old he weighed

For Lennox, a London tom, there was no choice but to switch to canned food, and he clearly liked it.

exactly 10 lbs – the ideal weight for a male cat with his frame.

Then a problem arose: his owner had to work out of town during the week and asked a neighbour to come in and feed Lennox. There was no choice but to switch to convenient, canned food. He clearly liked it, and it was difficult to entice him to eat fresh meals at the weekends. After only two months he weighed in at 12 lbs. The owner felt guilty – not as a result of his weight gain, but because of the obvious loneliness of the cat – and she persuaded a friend in the country to have him, who insisted that Lennox be neutered.

Lennox took a while to adjust to the outdoors and, despite leading a more active life, was getting fatter. He became finicky about food and only really liked one commercial brand. A visit to the vet put his weight at 14 lbs, which the vet explained was due to the neutering, but warned that it should be watched. The vet advised feeding him less food, or trying a diet food.

His new owner acknowledged that she had doubtless overfed him with the one food he fancied in order to gain his confidence and affection. Although she didn't like the sound of the vet's recommendation, she gave it a try. Lennox, however, didn't. He became thoroughly obstreperous, taking out most of his anger on the furniture. She then switched to serving him reasonable helpings of a formulated diet food twice a day which, after thirty-six hours of stubbornness, he ate in a desultory manner. He also rejected all attempts at friendship or play, simply sleeping or becoming a menace in the kitchen.

Clearly, she thought, there were only two options open to her: letting him become a big, fat, unhealthy cat eating the food he liked, or giving him back. Lennox's future looked bleak, but an article on naturopathic vets that she read came to his rescue. 'It's the alternative clinic for you, my boy', he was firmly told. And there she was given what sounded like sensible advice on Lennox's nutritional requirements and behaviour. The strategy was to introduce fresh foods gradually into his preferred nosh, aiming to eliminate the processed products within a month. Once the switch to natural food had been accepted by the cat, then desirable quantities could be worked out. Lennox reached his target weight of 10 lbs within eight months. The quantity of food served to him was not reduced, but divided into three meals, each consisting of a generous tablespoon. This suited Lennox, and he is now content.

3: Dandolo

Dandolo is a marmalade-coloured, pure-bred Persian cat, with a long, luxurious coat. He looks huge, but when he is picked up he is actually suprisingly light; underneath all that fur is an agile body, and you can feel his ribs. But this wasn't always the case: eighteen months ago he weighed 21 lbs. Now he is 13 lbs, which is just about right for his large frame.

Persians are prone to plumpness, and don't like to exert themselves too much. Although Dandolo lives in a city flat with a large terrace, he has always been more inclined to snooze in the sun rather than run around the available space. His owner automatically fed him the brand of commercial food that had been recommended by the breeder. He had initially offered Dandolo milk, but it made the cat sick. Occasionally he made the effort to serve his cat fresh liver or fish, but Dandolo only sniffed around it. So the usual, commercial nosh became the cat's daily fare. Dandolo was neutered at eight months.

Dandolo, a pure-bred Persian, loved to snooze on the terrace. His weight shot up to 21 lbs. It took over a year of his new, natural diet to reduce his weight to 13 lbs. He still has to be bullied into taking exercise.

Dandolo put on weight slowly but steadily over the next five years, without arousing his owner's concern. Later he admitted that he must have been blind, particularly since he was fastidious about grooming his cat daily. Dandolo's looks were a top priority, and everyone remarked on the beauty of the cat. He appeared to be healthy and content, and was certainly affectionate. His visits to the vet for periodic inoculations brought no adverse comments or warnings about his weight.

It therefore came as quite a shock when, following a change of vet, the owner was severely reprimanded for allowing Dandolo to get so heavy. A thorough examination and medical tests revealed heart and liver problems, and the owner was astonished to learn that his cat weighed 21 lbs, making him more than 30 per cent overweight. Dandolo was lucky to have fallen into the hands of a vet who considered bad nutrition to be the main cause of degenerative disease.

Drastic changes were recommended. Dandolo found himself having to eat freshly prepared food and a high percentage of raw food. He was stubborn for four days, and then came around. The plan was to feed him six small, but nourishing, high-protein meals a day. No snacks, no biscuits. It would be a long haul and involved the co-operation of the neighbours. If the food was not eaten immediately, it was taken away. True to cat form, Dandolo soon adapted to the new regimen. His weight was checked every month, and he averaged a 2 to 3 oz loss per week. After six months, the number of his daily meals was reduced to four, and the portions were slightly increased. After a year, he was down to three meals, and today he has two: ample servings (two tablespoons) of prime nutrients – liver, beef, chicken, fish, cheese, cooked grains and chopped vegetables – in the morning and evening.

The dietary change was tough on the owner, too, for he had to persevere and organise the feedings. Now, having returned to a manageable timetable, he's more than relieved, and is also very happy with Dandolo's health. Needless to say, Dandolo's coat is even more luxuriant, but he still lies around a lot and has to be bullied into taking exercise. The natural food, however, keeps his weight stable and his metabolism in fine order.

4: Cleo

Cleo is a female Siamese, agile and active at six years old. Her optimum weight is 7 lbs, and she has more or less maintained this for the past three years by means of a natural diet of three meals a day and the occasional, home-made, crunchy snack. She is a greedy cat, who grew up accustomed to feeding at will on both canned and dried food.

After she had had her first litter, she was neutered and then put on 4 lbs over eighteen months, which was a lot for her small frame. Her owner, who liked the idea of a more cuddly cat, wasn't displeased with her weight gain, and Cleo still dashed around in the Siamese way and so appeared fit. The switch to natural foods in her diet came about in a strange, and unintentional, way. Cleo's owner became pregnant and, almost from the beginning of her pregnancy, felt unbearably nauseous whenever she opened a can of cat food; she could no longer cope with the smell. So Cleo, by a quirk of fate, was put on a more natural nutritional diet.

Good food was now an important issue for the mother-to-be, as she was also putting on too much weight. She gave up snacks and her habit of eating a large evening meal and took to preparing four small, nutritious meals a day. Cleo, too, reaped the benefit of these fresh, natural ingredients, for she ate more or less the same food as her mistress, and at the same time.

At first Cleo made a fuss about the dietary change, but was eventually won over by enjoying the treat of receiving four offerings a day, more or less hand-fed. (The previous routine had consisted of morning and evening feeds). Clearly, the increased attention paid to her made up for the switch in foods. Fortunately, the diet was high in protein, but her owner in any case wisely checked with an animal nutritionist as she was nervous about any lack of essential nutrients contained in Cleo's new diet. She was very surprised to learn that although Cleo was getting enough protein, she was probably short of fats, which should comprise 25 per cent of the feline diet. Her owner was on a low-fat regimen, so some changes had to be made. Cleo, however, had no intention of giving up the new-found bliss of sharing meal times with her owner. Small adjustments provided the perfect compromise, however.

Grilled fish and salad for her owner became flaked fish mixed with cream or butter for Cleo; she also got the skin and fatty bits of roast chicken. A sandwich of sardines or tuna contained lettuce and tomato for the future mother, and a good spread of butter for Cleo. Fresh, raw, chopped liver was added to some meals, while egg dishes, such as cheese omelette, were shared. Cleo also developed a taste for healthy oat flapjacks – home-made ones were permitted on her owner's diet (see the special recipe for cats on page 99).

After nine months this dietary plan had become Cleo's way of life, though her meals were reduced to three a day, each comprising a tablespoon of mixed food with a formulated daily vitamin-and-mineral supplement. The most significant result was her loss of all the previously added pounds with no apparent effect. She also gained a sleeker, shinier coat.

The good news is that she never returned to canned and dried foods, and to date has not gained weight. The bad news is that she insists on eating at the same time and in the same place as the rest of the household, hence the three-meals-a-day routine, and the need to ban her from the dining-room when there are guests.

Cleo, a female Siamese, had the good fortune to be put on a natural diet when her owner became pregnant and felt nauseous opening canned food.

5: Maurice

Maurice is a Maine Coon who enjoys the brisk climate of Ithaca, New York State. He's an indoor-outdoor cat, but is not inclined to roam further than the territorial limits of his garden patch. He is seven years old and neutered. He belongs to one of the biggest breeds, but when Maurice weighed in at 22 lbs – considered the top end of the optimum scale – two years ago, the vet announced that he was much too heavy for his medium-sized frame. He was sentenced to losing a target 14 lbs within a year, at 4 oz per week a tough order.

Maine Coons may experience a specific health problem if they become overweight, hence the urgent need for Maurice to lose weight. The American vet, Greg G Keller, of the Orthopedic Foundation for Animals in Columbia, Missouri, points to a recent evaluation, which showed that approximately 25 per cent of Maine Coons develop hip dysplasia.

The local vet recommended a reduction of food and an increase in fibre. This did not suit Maurice's temperament at all. He had been used to two large bowls of canned food a day, as well as snacks and a continuous supply of dried food. The whole household was affected by his irritation, and after a month his weight was still the same. His owners were baffled until he was discovered sneaking next door, where he was indulged with treats.

His owners decided to take matters into their own hands and follow their common sense, also taking advice from the new genre of naturopathic cat books. They came up with this plan: Maurice would be fed four meals a day, at 8 am, 12 pm, 4 pm and 8 pm. They prepared a single mixture per day, comprising 45 per cent of protein and 30 per cent of fat (usually contained in meat, chicken or fish), the balance being made up with grains and vegetables. Maurice got one tablespoon of this per meal and nothing in between – certainly no snacks.

From the start, he was fed a wide variety of proteins, the goal being that eventually the basis of Maurice's meals would be formed from whatever the family was eating. His preferred protein was poultry – chicken, duck and Cornish hens – the skin and fat, as well as the lean meat. A beef casserole went down well, but he was

finicky about fish and wouldn't touch sardines or tuna. He liked liver only when it was lightly cooked, yet lapped up fresh, raw, ground beef when it was mixed with an egg yolk and a few rolled oats. Although he developed somewhat odd culinary tastes, they were consistent. Maurice's menu range was established within three weeks, and his owners rotated a selection of seven dishes.

Even the big-eating Maurice seemed satisfied, and made less fuss about the change of diet than he had about reducing the quantity of his usual food. It took fourteen months to get his weight down to the target figure, and he has managed to maintain it by continuing to eat home-made meals – now down to two substantial ones in the morning and evening – plus the occasional extra titbit of cheese or specially baked crunchies. It looks as though he'll avoid that hip problem!

Maurice, a Maine Coon, took to sneaking next door to supplement what he regarded as an unsatisfactory dietary change.

4 Are aerobics really necessary?

The answer to the question posed in the title is a definite 'yes', but only to a certain degree, and not in the way that we associate aerobics with physical jerks. There's a great difference between the cat's anatomy, with its inbred and instinctive mental-muscular processes, and our own, more restricted, physical structure and calculated behaviour.

For a start, cats are incapable of sustaining effort, so forget a go-for-the-burn routine, for your cat might literally fry. This is because if it does low-key exercise, such as trotting, the energy it uses is more than that of a dog of the same weight, and if this effort is continued the muscular system generates so much power that the cat's body will overheat. The cat's metabolism is geared so that even after less than a minute of hyper-energy expenditure it has to stop and pant.

There is no way that cats can be endurance athletes. They are stalkers not walkers; they don't stroll, they sprint; they leap and pounce. When revved up they can actually reach a speed of 48 kph (30 mph) in a few seconds, which is sometimes evident when you see them dashing around the house.

All cats are capable of concentrated spurts of energy, and can move their bodies in amazing ways. Size and breed make no difference because, as a species, cats have yet to produce significant anatomical extremes.

There are three main body types: lithe, muscular and cobby. The lithe cats are mostly of oriental and Mediterranean origin; both pure-breds and mongrels have long bodies, narrow shoulders, slim and longish legs and triangular faces. The muscular felines have sturdier-looking shoulders and rumps, medium-length legs and strong, rounded heads; these are found living in colder and more

There are three main feline body types: lithe, muscular and cobby.

SOME CAT FACTS

The cat's super-muscular body gives it the capacity to twist and turn in an impressive variety of ways, from a languorous stretch to the rapid strides of the chase. It can also clear up to five times its own height and turn its back into an inverted 'U'. There is simply no excuse for immobility in a cat.

challenging surroundings and are invariably the biggest cats. The cobby cat is solidly built and somewhat cuddly, with thick legs and a rounded, flattish face; it is the everyman's and every-country cat.

Whatever your cat's type, it still has more than five hundred separate skeletal muscles, the largest driving the powerful hind legs. Compare that figure to the considerably larger human body, which has around six-hundred-and-fifty muscles, and you'll understand why the cat boasts the flexibility of a contortionist, or at least why it should do.

A BODY BUILT FOR ACTION

The cat is unique, in that it has managed to emerge from countless aeons of evolution with its inherent and extraordinary combination of power, flexibility and balance intact. I know it's hard to believe when you look at your pet when it is curled up by the fire, on the couch or basking in the sun. That cat – your cat – actually has the capability to do a lot, but is not too keen on letting you know it these days. Its basic body equipment will, however, allow it to perform a work-out equal to that of a lion or a tiger.

Why is it so agile and powerful? Because the cat has both an adapted skeleton and a specialised cellular system within its muscles. Firstly, the feline backbone possesses twenty-six more vertebrae than the human equivalent. These flexible bones are held

together by muscles rather than ligaments – unlike in humans – which give your cat a range of agility unknown to us.

Cats also have a unique shoulder arrangement, in that the top of the spinal skeletal structure is free of rigid bone restrictions. The muscles are therefore in control at this vital pivotal point, and thus freely enable a wide range of movements. Perhaps the most significant feline feature in terms of movement is the shoulders' anatomical connection to the forelegs, which give cats the capacity to move in many directions. This means that cats can stretch, lengthen their stride, or twist and turn almost at will.

Cats aren't made for walking. This feline predator instinctively knows that it has to save its strength for the sudden dash and final charge. Cats do, however, qualify for certain finals in athletic competition: medals are theirs for the taking in the leap, pounce and jump categories. They are no mean sprinters either, and can go from zero to unbelievable speeds within seconds. They are also specialists of spring, uncoiling their muscles in a flash. And no matter where they are coming from or going to, they have an innate sense of balance: cats always land on their feet. Clearly, this is a body that can do much more than most – it just doesn't like doing it that often. It prefers to sleep.

MUST CATS SLEEP SO MUCH?

Rest reassured, your cat is not unique in sleeping away two-thirds of its life. It's not caused by laziness, but is instead a genetically programmed, biological need. If your cat appears to be comatose for more than sixteen hours of the day, however, you have a problem. (Not that it's easy to monitor your cat's sleeping pattern if you are out for most of the day, as cats are quite capable of indulging in complete inertia when they are on their own and then springing to attention when the door-key enters the lock. All we can be sure of is that they certainly haven't done the housework in our absence.)

THE CATNAP SYNDROME

Cats sleep more than any other mammal, and no one knows why. They are certainly experts in this, and possess the enviable ability to drop off apparently at will. A feline insomniac is unknown. The daily quota of sleep varies (though not much) according to the

season, weather, environment, hunger, sexual urges and age. Kittens and old cats sleep more than healthy adults.

The natural pattern of feline sleep consists of a number of short catnaps within a twenty-four-hour cycle (the latter is known as circadian rhythm and is controlled by an internal biological clock which causes the mind and body to interact and determines times of activity and rest).

Doubtless you are only too aware that your cat's body timetable is at odds with your own. Cats are at their most alert at dawn and when the sun goes down – it's that inherited hunting instinct again – and are sleepiest in the middle of the day or night. They generally find it hard to alter this embedded behaviour, but some cats with working owners have been known to sleep away the entire day and

Cats are at their most alert at dawn.

then be extra-eager for fun and games in the morning and evening. This gives you a chance to take advantage of such enthusiasm and initiate a bit of feline body-training.

Sleep is induced by the external factors of warmth and a full stomach; internally, it is triggered by a chemical – melatonin – which is released in the brain and is thought to be responsible for the regular rhythms that govern a cat's sleeping pattern. A cats first falls into a light sleep, and then sinks into a deeper state, relaxing completely and most probably dreaming. After six to seven minutes of deep sleep, it will return to twenty to thirty minutes of light sleep. It is thus only dead to the world for a very short span of time, so don't be fooled: your cat can be prodded into action at most times.

THE GREAT STRETCH

On waking from sleep, the first thing that a fit cat does is to stretch, flexing its muscles, arching its back and extending its limbs to their limits. This stimulates its circulation and tones up both its nervous and muscular systems. In fact, humans could learn a thing or two from this revitalising stretch after sleep and, indeed, advocates of yoga have done so: their 'salute to the sun' sequence of early-morning exercise closely mimics the cat's natural stretching.

A fat cat will make only a half-hearted effort to perform this vital physical exertion. A reluctance to stretch properly is an early indicator of overweight – even when obesity is not that obvious to the eye – and is a warning signal that you've got to persuade your cat to eat less and exercise more.

LETTING OFF STEAM

All cat-owners know the unnerving experience of witnessing their cat suddenly dashing around the house as though it's been struck by a bolt from heaven or has trodden on an exposed electric wire. The cat will fling itself hither and thither at top speed, and then, after a few minutes, will screech to a halt on all paws, whereupon it will dissolve into a calm, contented heap and settle down to indulge in a bit of washing.

This is perfectly normal behaviour for a healthy indoor cat and is officially known as 'vacuum activity'. One doesn't need a degree in veterinary science to work out that a confined cat – whose ancestors have passed on the instinct to stalk, pounce and overwhelm its prey – must store up an awful lot of energy just sitting around a comfortable home. There comes a time when all this pent-up capacity to catch and kill has to find an outlet, otherwise the cat will either pop or end up on the psychiatrist's couch – and some have done so. We all need a frenzied burst of activity from time to time, and your cat is no exception.

The time to worry – that is, when you have got over the irritation of having your house torn apart – is when your cat has fewer such fits, or none. Being apathetic means that it is not storing up energy, and that something is therefore basically wrong. This could be a serious problem, such as a disease or infection, but it could be simply that your cat is overweight and that any lack of incentive to exercise through play has made it moribund. If this is the case it is entirely your fault, and you have to do something about it.

MIND OVER MATTER

Cats have a bad reputation when it comes to their amenability to being trained. It's not that they don't have the brains to understand and comply with you, but rather that for some perverse reason they prefer to follow their own ideas.

Unlike dogs, praise is not enough to induce a cat to perform some accomplishment; cats demand a reward – one that can be eaten. If you want to be a serious trainer of felines, you'd better have a store of snacks and tasty titbits to hand. Bribery is therefore the only way in which you can get your cat to go through the leaps and bounds of an assault course (see pages 62–63). And you will furthermore need a huge amount of patience in order slowly to show your cat what you have in mind, and then to reward it out of all proportion to its actual achievement.

Start with a stick. If you put it on the ground, the odds are that your cat will walk around it. (Somehow it doesn't occur to the feline mind that making a little jump would be easier.) Raise the stick slightly and simultaneously entice your cat with a bit of sardine and it will eventually get the message: it'll jump to get the food. You can do all sorts of things with a stick – raise it, or make it act as a hoop, for example – but only reward your cat for good and proper jumps. Research shows that cats only remember tasks if they get something out of it. Is this a big con trick?

THE ROLE OF PLAY

We can achieve something here. Cats adore games – chasing balls, strings, jingly-jangly things, and so forth. This is the best way to get that fat cat to exercise. It thinks it's playtime, but you know it's a serious work-out.

Ten to twenty minutes of play a day can keep your cat fit and healthy. In fact, this is about the limit of your cat's attention span. Much as it loves your devotion to throwing and trailing, its concentration and interest gradually wane. Once you find yourself doing the retrieving, stop.

DID YOU KNOW?

Your cat will benefit greatly from even a short work-out. Apart from the obvious improvement that it will make to its muscle tone and circulation, it also helps to regulate the cat's appetite and aids its digestion. And did you know that the cat's brain demands a great deal of energy? Although it accounts for less than 1 per cent of the cat's body weight, it requires 20 per cent of the blood pumped by the heart. This means that if you set difficult tasks for your cat to perform it will first have to do a bit of thinking and will thus use up as much energy in its head as in its muscles.

SOME CAT FACTS

Don't worry about your cat overdoing it in the sports arena; cats instinctively prefer to work through stealth – favouring a wait-and-see attitude that may (or may not) end up in a pounce. In other words, cats will avoid doing too much exercise for its own sake and wouldn't dream of becoming overheated. Their sweat glands are restricted to the bare skin on the underside of their paws and around their mouths, noses and nipples.

Cats prefer fun and games to formal exercise programmes – even chasing their shadows on the ground or reflections from the TV screen constitute a good game.

There is no age limit to play. Kittens, of course, are naturals, but cats of any age will happily play with the simplest of things. Even if you can't persuade your cat to do more advanced aerobics, a play session every day will tone its muscles, strengthen its cardiovascular system, reduce stress and alleviate boredom.

A WALK ON THE WILD SIDE

In theory, you can train a cat to walk on a leash. In practice, I have never managed to achieve it. I doubt if too many others have either, for I have yet to see a cat happily enjoying a tethered walk.

For what it's worth, this is the standard procedure if you want to try to walk your cat. Cats shouldn't have leads as such; they require a harness that tucks under their tums. It's the very devil to get on, but practiced cat-trainers say that before you attempt that you should first nonchalantly leave the harness lying around the house for the cat to smell and play around with. Then comes that dreadful moment of putting the harness on. No matter how familiar the cat has become with this contraption, my experience is that it still objects to being tied up.

The next step is to let your cat move around the house in its harness. It may – or may not – be happy to do so. If you and your cat manage to pass this hurdle, out you go – and good luck! I have found that cats have no inclination to stroll. They either sit stubbornly still or make a frantic beeline for any convenient cover. They hate cars, people, pavements, noise and anything alien.

THE CORNER GYM

Cats are naturally very playful, skilled climbers and like to leap around chasing after things, but they need to be given the opportunity to do so: the right place, the right equipment and the right enticements.

It is house-bound cats that really need to be stirred into action (though outdoor cats can benefit, too), and in the interests of both their satisfaction and your peace of mind about your precious furniture, they need their own space in which to exercise.

Don't panic, this does not mean that you have to allocate a separate room to your cat. So much can be done within the confines of a corner, which can be cleverly camouflaged so that it's not a blot on your interior décor (as are most manufactured scratching- and climbing-posts) and which will give your cat its much-required privacy, as well as a veritable gymnasium of equipment and a nursery of toys. Remember that cats are not show-offs, unlike dogs. They prefer to do many of their tricks surreptitiously, and also like to view you from a high, hidden place. The cat's corner is ideal for enabling both exercise and stealth.

This is a plan for a fully equipped fitness centre, in which your cat can engage in work-outs without being coerced to do so. It is disguised as a play and observation area, and provides a variety of beneficial activities. You'll need the following basics.

A ladder: prop up a small ladder at an angle across a corner; attach triangular shelves to the walls to adjoin a couple, or all, of the ladder's rungs; cover the shelves with spare pieces of carpet. Bind the sides and shelf-free rungs of the ladder with strong, webbed cloth (ordinary floor cloths work well), sacking or bits of flexible carpet. This revamped ladder is now a climbing- and scratching-post, while the shelves encourage jumps and leaps, as well as acting as secluded observation spots.

Mobiles: attach a selection of balls and toys to the sides and rungs of the ladder, using string, wire or springs. Cats adore things that dangle and sparkle, and will instinctively stretch and leap to grasp a moving object. Vary the lengths so that there's always a mobile within reach, no matter where the cat sits. These will keep your cat occupied, amused and active when you're away from home.

A well-trained mother will encourage her kittens to incorporate the corner gym into their daily routine from the beginning of their lives.

SOME CAT FACTS

The cat is genetically programmed to be a lithe and athletic creature. It needs exercise and enjoys it. Agility is essential to a healthy life. However, house-bound cats do not seem to have the necessary get-up-and-go with which to organise themselves to take action. It is up to you to provide toys and climbing-posts, make time for play and patiently show your cat how to get its act together in order to do a bit of training on its own.

A house tree: place a large, indoor tree – this can be living or artificial – in a substantial pot in front of the ladder. If the tree is flimsy, tie it to a sturdy, wooden 'trunk' (obtained from a lumberyard or garden centre) which you have embedded securely in the pot. In order to prevent your cat using the soil as a litter tray, it is a good idea to cover its surface with cardboard or wood. The tree should all but hide the ladder, and will bring a fresh, decorative touch to your room. As for cats, they love the feel of the branches and leaves, and will also use the trunk support as an aid for scratching and climbing.

BASIC FITNESS TRAINING

A work-out of just ten to twenty minutes a day will go a long way towards getting your cat fit and trim – and towards maintaining that condition. This can be done through playing under your direction. The aim is to get your cat to stretch, pounce, leap and jump as much as possible within that time span. There's no point in considering a longer period of play, thinking it to be more beneficial, as most cats' attention wanders and you'll find yourself doing all the work for a bemused feline spectator. Devise a repertoire of games, but do each only a few times. Too much repetition bores cats and they become indifferent and lazy. Here are some suggestions.

Freely bouncing balls: small rubber or ping-pong balls are the best. Cats will eagerly chase them around a room, down the stairs and around and under furniture. When they are bounced high, many cats will jump up to swipe or catch them.

Things on strings: the most enticing are balls, catnip mice, cotton reels, feathers (pulled from a standard feather-duster) or spiders made from pipe-cleaners. You can more or less dictate your cat's movements by the way in which you entice it. Drag the thing-on-a-string along the ground, starting and stopping as you do so, and your cat will leap or pounce on it. Dangle it in the air, and your cat will jump up to retrieve it. Move it around on a table and your cat will spring up to still it. Play hide-and-seek around corners, behind cushions and curtains, and your cat will enthusiastically stalk and pounce on it.

A hanging rope: this should be both sturdy and tasselled at the end. It can be hung from a banister or from a hook sited at the top of a door frame. It should terminate a couple of feet from the floor to make the cat stretch to pull or play with it. Many cats will happily play with the rope on their own, but no cat can resist attempting contact if you swing it back and forth; swing it hard and high to force your cat to perform a major stretch.

Scrunched-up foil: cats love the shine and crackle of foil, and a simple, hand-made ball of kitchen foil can keep your cat on the go for quite a while before it tires of the game.

Paper bags and newspaper: by simply moving a stick under a paper bag or sheets of newspaper you can set your cat on high alert as a result of the noise and action; it'll watch and wait for only a few seconds, then pounce and frantically rummage around to try to nail the cause.

A stick or fly-swatter: you can gradually train your cat to jump over these, but a reward is absolutely necessary, in the form of a small nibble of its favourite food. What is more, this should be given immediately after a successful performance. First put the stick on the floor and show your cat how to walk over it in order to get at the tasty morsel on the other side. (A cat's natural inclination is to walk around it.) Raise the stick by degrees, and your cat will finally get the message that it has to jump for its reward. Watch out, though, because once the stick reaches your cat's height it will be sneaky and try to dash underneath – then the food has to be held high and only brought down after a successful jump.

A hoop: yes, you can teach cats to jump through hoops, from the floor and from a height to the floor. Again, training your cat to do so is a slow and gradual process, which can only be achieved with the lure of reward. Start by holding the hoop on the floor and easing your cat through it to show it what you have in mind. Raise it by degrees, and then graduate to getting your cat to jump from a chair, through the hoop and on to the floor – and also *vice versa*. This is a good work-out.

THE ASSAULT COURSE

This is where imagination, patience and stamina come into their own – yours, rather than your cat's. Felines are capable of going through all sorts of up-and-down constructions at considerable speed, employing skilful, athletic manoeuvres in the process. They also have the intelligence to work out twists and turns and entrances and exits, but only if there's an edible goal at the end of the tunnel. Receiving your praise is a pleasing bonus, but you will have to accept from the start that this not your cat's primary objective in complying with your wishes.

The idea is to assemble what amounts to an obstacle race from items that can be easily stored in a cupboard, together with pieces of furniture that are immune to a bit of rough treatment: sturdy cardboard boxes, wooden planks, small tree-trunks, flexible bits of cardboard to roll into tubes, any wide plastic tubes, expandable wood trellises, ladders, stools, kitchen chairs and lengths of rope, for example.

Plan your assembly line in a practical way, in other words, make sure that you can put it together and dismantle it in a few minutes. And stick to the final result: cats get confused if you keep altering the course. However, do not construct the entire line-up expecting your cat to nose its way through this strange labyrinth first time around. You will have to introduce your cat to the obstacles in stages, adding the next hurdle only when the former ones have become familiar. All this takes time, and you will initially have to offer a reward after your cat has completed each section of the course, enticing it all the way. Only after many weeks will your cat understand that it has to get to the end of the line before it receives that special treat. Believe it or not, cats enjoy this form of exercise, and – as all owners well know – they simply wouldn't comply if they didn't.

1 Place a cardboard box with circles cut out on two opposite sides on a stool or kitchen chair and provide access by means of a small log or lower-level chair. Entice your cat (with a reward of food, of course) into the box – it can easily jump out from either side.

2 Cut a circle in one side of another cardboard box, and then open and lower the flap on another side. Place the box on a higher stool, chair or table. Join it to the previous obstacle with a plank and get your cat to pass through the familiar section. Reward your cat and then encourage it to cross the plank into the next box, rewarding it again when it has done so.

3 Roll a piece of flexible cardboard into a tunnel and place it on the floor within jumping distance of the flap-down box. Attach a shiny object, ball or mouse to a string or stick and wiggle it around at the tunnel entrance; pull it through when your cat jumps down to capture it and reward your cat on its exit.

5 Getting the diet right

I know this sounds obvious, but the most important fact to imprint on your mind regarding the feline diet is that a cat is not a dog, and cannot live off table scraps. All right, perhaps cats did so once upon a time, but that was when our meals were heartier, meatier, fresher and practically devoid of commercially processed foods. Most cats also had access to the outdoors, and therefore had opportunities to supplement any left-overs with a nutritious mouse or two. Today things are quite different, and even if we are short-sighted enough not to provide ourselves with healthy food, it's not fair to deprive our cats of the vital, natural nutrients that are so important to them.

Unlike humans and dogs, cats are not omnivores who are able to digest and utilise both plant and animal matter. They are strict carnivores and their protein requirement is very high – roughly twice that of a dog's. In addition, cats are unable to manufacture some essential amino acids for themselves, and so have to acquire them second-hand through the flesh of another animal who can. The most significant of these is taurine, an amino-acid derivative, which research has only recently identified. It is vital for your cat's eyesight and also protects against reproduction problems and heart failure. It is found in mice, meat, chicken, fish and eggs. There is little – if any – in plants. It is now routinely added to most commercial cat foods.

The importance of taurine is cited by many veterinarians and pet-food manufacturers as the deciding factor in favour of feeding cats commercial products as opposed to home-made diets. In other words, it is implied that owners are incapable of feeding their cats a properly balanced meal. Yet countless generations of healthy cats have thrived on the remains of the natural foods that we once used to eat. And who knows what so-called 'essential' element has still to be discovered? Today's scientifically formulated, 'complete' foods may very well lack a vital substance found in nature, but not yet manufactured in the laboratory.

A QUESTION OF BALANCE

We are forever hearing about the importance of 'perfect balance', in fact so much so that it's enough to make us become unnecessarily anxious about the adequacy of home-made food. But we shouldn't be. First of all, there is no ideal diet for all cats under all conditions. Secondly, there is no need for every single bowl of food that you feed your cat to be packed with all the essentials: the inclusion of these can be spread over many days. It doesn't make sense to jam everything into every meal, and, indeed, it could even be detrimental if your cat is eating the same food all the time.

A varied, natural diet will provide the best-quality nutrients to maintain your cat's health and fuel an efficient metabolism. Learning how to create a balanced diet is actually very straightforward and not nearly as complicated as many animal nutritionists would have us believe.

Admittedly, we can certainly benefit from scientific dietary analysis and research (which is primarily sponsored by the pet-food industry) by looking for the essential elements that they have named from the three food groups – protein, fat and carbohydrate – in natural sources.

WHAT PERCENTAGE OF EACH?

Protein is the prime nutrient. Researchers can't resist coming up with a minimum figure necessary for health, which, for an inactive, house-bound cat, they say is 21 per cent of its daily food intake. In the wild, however, it is about 47 per cent and naturopathic veterinarians estimate the healthy ideal for the adult domestic cat to be 35 to 45 per cent.

The amount of fat in a cat's diet should be between 20 and 35 per cent (some natural nutritionists say that it can safely go as high as 40 per cent). It should be noted that growing kittens need up to 50 per cent protein and 35 percent fat. The balance is made up of carbohydrates – plant matter.

SOME CAT FACTS

Taurine is an amino-acid derivative that is vital for good eyesight and the maintenance of the heart muscles. Cats, unlike other animals, cannot make it from ingested protein, so it has to come pre-formed from an animal source or be given as a supplement. It can be found in most health-food shops in capsule form, which can be easily opened and the contents then sprinkled on food or used in prepared dishes.

CONCENTRATE ON THE FRESH

Personally, I prefer to give my cat completely fresh, home-made meals, but I am also a realist: it is convenient – and at times even unavoidable – to use processed products. An acceptable healthy compromise is to combine these with natural foods to make interesting and nourishing dishes, but keep them to a minimum. If your cat has been reared on canned and dried food, it is often difficult to wean it onto natural meals and the new diet therefore has to be introduced slowly.

HOW MUCH, HOW OFTEN?

Although this book makes recommendations as to the amount of food that cats should be fed, it should be remembered that all cats are individuals, and that there can thus be no definitive guide as to quantity. The size and number of a cat's daily meals depend on its age, weight, breed, temperament and condition.

In general, moggies need more food than pure-breds. Climate also plays a part: cats living in hot climates eat less than those in cold ones. By the same token, indoor cats who are coddled with central heating and blazing fires should not be fed a lot as they certainly don't need any extra fat to insulate them. What shouldn't vary, however, is the ratio of protein, fat and carbohydrate, as indicated in the 'What percentage of each?' section above. The high

SOME CAT FACTS

Hot or cold food? Which is best? Neither. Most cats prefer luke-warm dishes served at a temperature ranging between 25°C and 40°C (77°F and 104°F). So allow hot, cooked food to cool down and never serve a meal directly from the refrigerator.

SOME CAT FACTS

Raw or cooked? This is a debatable issue. Pure naturalists say that raw flesh is the only correct food to feed your cat. But today this can contain harmful bacteria and enzymes. If you can find absolutely fresh meat of the best quality, cats can safely enjoy a treat of raw, minced beef. Otherwise it's best to cook all meats, poultry and fish lightly. There is a specific problem with raw fish, for it contains thiaminases, enzymes which destroy the essential vitamin thiamine (B1). Grains must always be cooked, but some vegetables can be finely grated or minced and served raw, provided that they are mixed with other ingredients.

nutritional quality of food has to remain constant, while the size of the portions that you feed your cat has to be worked out according to your cat's specific circumstances.

The correct amount of food that you should give your cat is determined by its energy content, which is measured in kilocalories (kcals). The calorie equation that is so familiar to us applies as much to cats as to humans, so in order to maintain your cat's steady weight level the veterinary advice is that you mustn't feed your cat more calories than it's likely to expend, otherwise it'll get fat. This is true, but may not give you the full picture, warn naturopathic practitioners. Beware of those 'empty' calories provided by junk food: although they provide energy, they also contain toxins which in themselves could cause the accumulation of extra fatty deposits.

In scientific parlance, an adult cat needs about 50 kcals per 450 g/1 lb of its body weight per day. (You can go mad working out the sums, for a cat's daily energy requirement can range from as little as 125 kcals up to 580, and often even more for a pregnant or lactating female.)

How many meals should your cat eat a day? There is no hard-and-fast rule as regards this, though the norm is typically twice a day, with free access to nibbles. This regimen, however, is not ideal, and has been primarily adopted to suit our own working hours and consciences. But we are thereby doing our cats a disservice and making them into fat felines. Naturopathic animal nutritionists point out that three smaller meals a day both help to maintain a cat's optimum weight, and also provide the most effective way in which to attain gradual and safe fat loss. If you are out all day, the answer is to supply your cat with breakfast, an early evening meal and a late supper. There is no problem if you are late or miss the middle meal; your cat will not suffer unduly and you can compensate for it at the next. You must, however, make sure that you cut out that ever-ready dried food.

THE TABLESPOON MEASURE

In actual food weight, a cat's energy requirement ranges from 225 g/8 oz to 375 g/13 oz. Perhaps it is easier to think in terms of the feline stomach capacity and give your cat two to three tablespoons of food at conveniently spaced intervals two or three times a day. Your cat will let you know if it's starving, and, at the other extreme, you'll soon see if it's putting on weight and can then adjust the portions accordingly. Just make sure that every calorie that goes into your cat is of nutritional value.

CATS EAT FOR ENERGY

When you look at your curled-up, snoozing cat you might find it hard to accept that its prime purpose in eating is to acquire energy, not to enjoy the good feeling that results from a full tum. What on

A cat's stomach is quite small, but it will not take kindly to reduced quantities of its normal food.

earth does it want energy for? A trot to the kitchen bowl and back? Old habits and genetic programming die hard, and the cat's well-established metabolic system hasn't quite caught up with its new, comfortable life.

Animal experts inform us that cats eat until their energy requirements are met. I believe that this is one of those statements that are correct in theory but do not always apply in life. It may also be true in the wild, but in our pampered house-pet we are looking at a radically different being.

Of course, all bodily activities require energy, and there's a lot going on inside that seemingly inert form. Cats use most of their energy simply to stay alive, to keep their hearts and circulations going, to metabolise food and to keep warn. Only a small amount of energy is used for growth, bodily repair and muscular activity. It seems to me, however, that today's house-cats haven't quite developed a revised monitoring system with which to judge the level of energy that they need. Surely many of them gobble up amounts of food that are far in excess of their anticipated activity.

One significant aspect of the energy equation that is rarely considered by owners is that in the natural state cats require a certain amount of energy to fuel their mental activity. The stalking and catching of prey demand plotting and planning, as well as physical prowess; an instinctively regulated energy intake took this into account. However, the metabolism and nervous system of today's pampered pet have not had time to adjust to the new way of feeding; most cats are fooled into thinking that they need more energy than they actually do. Of course, you can't make your cat use its mind more, but play certainly helps to stimulate a feline's thought processes.

Cats can't always be relied upon to get it right: it is up to us to take charge and exert control over the quantity of food that they consume. But that's not all. It is also very important to realise that, if this 'energy first' instinct still prevails, we must be sure that even the smallest portions of the food that we serve our cats contain vital nutrients. And if we are controlling the calories that our cats ingest in order to promote weight loss, it is even more relevant.

Fat provides the most calories – about 9 kcals per gram, or 250 kcals per ounce. Pure protein and carbohydrate each produce levels of 4 kcals per gram, or 110 kcals per ounce.

SOME CAT FACTS

Home-grown greens planted in pots or trays can provide indoor cats with the vegetation that they need. Feline favourites are cock's-foot or lawn grass, which can often be found pre-sown at pet shops. You can also sow such cereal grasses as wheat or oats. Pots have to be kept in a moist, warm and dark place until germination has occurred, and should then be placed in a light position. Cats love to nibble on the fresh, succulent leaves and even seem content just sniffing them. Once in the habit of eating or smelling them, they miss their greens if they are deprived of them, so in order to ensure a continuous supply sow a couple of pots every few weeks.

PROTEIN: FLESH IS BEST

Since time immemorial cats have positively thrived on tearing away at the bodies of smaller animals and then ingesting the lot. They don't know – or care – why they eat in this way, and it is modern scientists who have pinpointed the reasons that underlie this feeding behaviour.

The current theory is that the cat's liver possesses an enzyme system that requires a constant supply of protein to provide energy for its metabolism, body growth and repair. This may have to do with the fact that the cat's stomach empties very quickly after each meal – after all, it is extremely small.

Proteins are made up of simpler compounds called amino acids, each of which is considered essential for the metabolism and, indeed, life. The problem is that not all are found in every protein

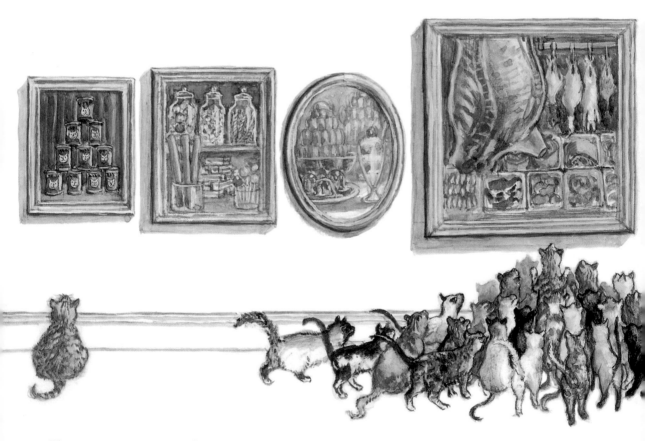

source, though some can be manufactured internally from vegetable matter; unfortunately, the cat is unique among mammals in not being able to do this. It is also highly likely there are still many more amino acids that have yet to be identified by scientists. The list enlarges as research progresses, so it is advisable to feed your cat a wide range of animal produce.

Although your cat converts most of its protein intake into energy, a certain amount must be used for its general physical maintenance, the reparation of cells and the digestive system. There is rarely any energy left over, but if there is it will be stored as a reserve supply of energy – as fat. Dietary protein, on the other hand, must always be replaced on a regular basis. There is no equivalent substitute.

It is, in fact, very difficult to feed too much protein to your cat,

Most cats know instinctively that the 'good proteins' are of benefit to their health. However, there are always exceptions to the rule: the cat at left can't see past the canned alternative, while the kittens on the right are drawn to the sweet, creamy cakes.

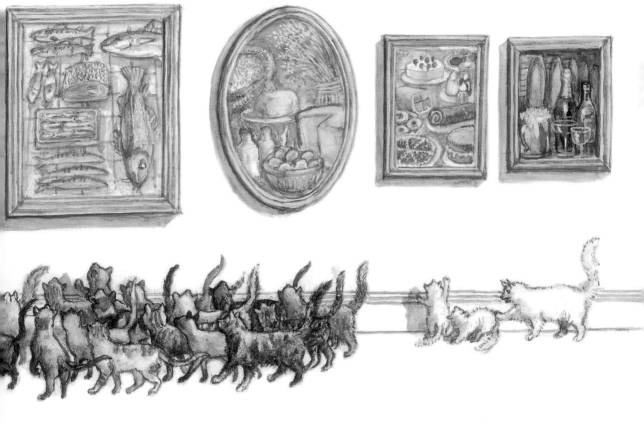

SOME CAT FACTS

Is liver the most perfect food for cats? Yes and no. Liver is the most nutritious food when served raw – and it can only be raw if it is fresh – as it is packed with protein, the right fats, vitamins and minerals. Cooking diminishes, and can even destroy, some of these nutrients. Too much liver, however, is bad. Any excess of the fat-soluble vitamins can become toxic. The most problematic is vitamin A which, if ingested at too high a level, can lead to impaired vision, skin rashes, hair loss and liver damage. A complete meal of liver should be limited to once or twice a week. If you want to serve it daily, it should comprise no more than a quarter of the day's total meals.

as long as the source and type is varied – too much of one kind of protein can cause problems. Cats are well equipped to deal with this prime nutrient, and a more common difficulty arises when the cat receives too little.

Variety is the key to both your cat's health and your convenience when providing its meals. The tale of a cat eating only one type of food is all too common. This is nutritional nonsense and, what's more, inexcusable behaviour on the part of the cat; no owner should stand for it. It is but an acquired habit with no biological foundation, yet one that is extremely difficult to break. Right from the start, kittens should be offered the whole spectrum of good proteins (see the chart opposite), and should you inherit a cat who is fixed in its ways, you will certainly have a tough time getting it to change. Although cats seem to delight in giving the impression that they'd rather starve than try an alternative food, if you are firm you'll finally win – albeit with a certain loss in the popularity stakes.

The ideal is to get to the stage when you are able to prepare most of your cat's food using your own daily protein selection as the basis for its meals. Vegetarians, of course, can't do this, and therefore have to be especially careful to provide their cats with enough of the right flesh protein; dairy products alone do not suffice.

Are there any foods that cats particularly like from the wide protein-containing range? Over the years I have found that poultry and game lead as the gourmet choices for all felines. I imagine that

What about fish? Fresh fish is excellent food and is loved by cats. It can only be fed raw if it has been freshly caught, otherwise it must be lightly cooked – steamed or baked. And it absolutely must be boned. Canned fish intended for human use is a reliable source as it doesn't contain harmful preservatives. Cats like salmon, sardines, mackerel, herring and tuna, but go easy on the tuna as it can contain a high proportion of polyunsaturated fats which destroy the valuable vitamin E. Also avoid all fish that has been canned in spicy or fancy sauces.

The good proteins

GAME FLESH:
venison, rabbit, wood pigeon, quail, pheasant and grouse

DOMESTIC ANIMAL FLESH:
beef, veal and lamb

ANIMAL ORGANS:
liver, kidney, tongue and heart

POULTRY:
turkey, chicken (particularly the liver), goose and duck

FISH:
salmon, sardine, mackerel, herring, tuna (limited),
cod and trout

DAIRY PRODUCTS AND EGGS:
egg yolk, Parmesan cheese, mozzarella, butter and milk
(preferably goat's or sheep's)

GRAINS (COOKED):
oats and unpolished rice

this is because the flesh is tender and easier to tear apart than the denser red meats. Pork and ham should be avoided, though a little crispy cured bacon is permitted, and goes down very well. Fish, of course, is both a favourite and very nutritious, but cats generally prefer substantial pieces and flakes of fish to the heads and tails; indeed, the head, with its tiny bones and teeth, can be hazardous. Fish, whether raw or cooked, should be boned.

The amount of good, natural protein contained in the diet greatly influences the cat's weight. The amount eaten will more or less equal the amount either used or excreted as waste. It is the excess ingestion of the wrong sorts of fats, starches and toxins that's responsible for the fat feline's curves and bulges.

Poultry and game are likely to be your cat's favourite proteins so get him started early on a diet which includes these meats.

FAT: CATS LOVE AND NEED IT

Cats are very lucky, in that they assimilate fat easily: unlike us, they can digest a high proportion of fat in their diet without necessarily putting on weight. Fat not only provides a concentrated source of energy, but also supplies essential fatty acids, acts as a carrier for the fat-soluble vitamins A, D, E and K and makes food tasty.

Fat should form up to 35 per cent of your cat's daily rations. This figure can go down to 20 per cent when your cat is on a slimming diet, but you should never cut it out altogether: feline health and low levels of fat are incompatible, and depriving your cat of fat could be positively dangerous.

Fats play a vital role in the production of substances that are integral to the metabolism. After absorption, they are broken down by enzymes into fatty acids and glycerol. Glycerol is the energy-giver, while the acids possess digestive and repair functions.

Linoleic, linolenic and arachidonic fatty acids are also essential to the cat's metabolism. Their names are impossible to recall, of course, but it is easy to remember that they must be eaten. The only source of all three is animal fat, though the first two can come from plant sources. Their metabolic role is but one very sound reason why the level of fat in a cat's diet should never go too low.

SOME FAT FACTS

Dietary fat contains vitamin A, and this has to be included in your cat's daily rations because cats cannot convert betacarotene – the plant source of vitamin A – into this very important metabolic element. Good sources of vitamin A include animal fats, liver and fish oils.

The good fats

DOMESTIC ANIMAL FLESH:
fat in the tissue of beef, lamb, chicken, duck and also in liver, kidney and tongue

DAIRY PRODUCTS AND EGGS:
egg yolk, Parmesan cheese, butter and milk (preferably goat's or sheep's)

OILS:
fish oils and olive oil

SOME FAT FACTS

Dairy products are good for your cat (but within limits), as the fat that they contain is a necessary carrier of very useful vitamins. All cats love fresh butter, so treat them to a dab every now and then. Soft, white cheeses are also of nutritional value – for example, mozzarella – while a little Parmesan adds taste and nutrients to many a dish. Avoid the hard, yellow cheeses made from cow's milk, and don't even consider margarine or substitute spreads.

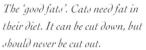
The 'good fats'. Cats need fat in their diet. It can be cut down, but should never be cut out.

CARBOHYDRATE: FIBRE OF VITAMIN AND MINERAL VALUE

Carbohydrates originate in plants, and include vegetables, fruits, grains and pulses. For millions of years the cat has obtained the benefit of their high vitamin and mineral content, not to mention the sun's energy, via the flesh and stomach contents of its prey.

Analytical scientists are quick to point out that there is no known carbohydrate requirement for the cat, because it gets sufficient energy from other sources. Naturopaths, on the other hand, are adamant that cats need some plant fibre to provide roughage, as well as to supply them with vitamins and minerals. In the wild, the cat obtains necessary roughage through the consumption of a whole animal or bird, including its fur or feathers. The domestic substitute is the cellulose fibre found in plants.

Carbohydrates are either sugars or starches, and, in order for your cat to be able use them, they have to be broken down into simple sugars. Cats, however, do not possess the micro-organisms with which to do this, so although you can serve your cat a few raw (grated) vegetables and fruits, the starches and grains have to be broken down through cooking.

An important point: excess starchy carbohydrate will be stored as fat, so it should be kept to a minimum within a cat's diet – just provide enough to supply your cat with extra nutrients and a little bit of roughage in order to aid excretion.

SOME CAT FACTS

Garlic is as good for cats as it is for us. It aids digestion, contributes to immunity and acts as an antioxidant. In addition, it is claimed to be particularly beneficial for a cat that is overweight, giving its metabolism a necessary kick-start. Include fresh garlic, very finely grated, in one meal a day – no more than a clove.

Your cat may need to be encouraged to include a tiny bit of carbohydrate in its diet. Always make sure that it is cooked before serving.

The good carbohydrates

GRAINS:
oats, wholewheat bread and brown rice

VEGETABLES:
dark-green leaf varieties, courgettes
(zucchini), carrots, beans, corn and potatoes

FRUIT:
bananas, apples, melons and berries

SUGAR:
molasses

WATER: THE REAL ESSENTIAL

Water is more than a nutrient: it is crucial to your cat's life, as it is to ours, but as a legacy of the cat's desert ancestry it is cleverer at water-conservation than we are. It has a remarkable ability to concentrate its urine in times of need, which accounts for that occasionally unpleasant, pungent aroma.

Despite this ability, your cat requires a considerable amount of water, most of which it gets from food. You should also ensure that fresh water is always available, however, particularly if you leave dry food around for your cat to eat at will. Cats also tend to drink at night – a behavioural flashback to those days in the desert.

The body of the cat comprises 60 per cent water, and even if it loses 10 per cent of this there can be dire problems. If the ratio goes down to 20 per cent the cat is close to dying: that's how essential water is.

Water is necessary for many things: it is the body's prime solvent and the main component of blood. It eases the transportation of blood, nutrients, antibodies and waste, aids digestion and influences kidney function and urine production. Water also regulates body temperature, although cats don't perspire through their skin. Water is evaporated via the lungs, urine and faeces. The pads of the paws can perspire, but if your cat is really hot it will pant.

THE HIDDEN LIFE-SAVERS: VITAMINS AND MINERALS

Vitamins and minerals are not foods as such, for they provide neither energy nor body-maintenance nutrients, but they are vital nevertheless. They help regulate the cat's metabolism and are integral parts of many body structures. Deficiencies of these substances can cause stunted growth, can slow down cellular repair, can cause muscular problems, a lowered immune system and malfunction of the digestive network.

In nature, cats acquire vitamins and minerals through consuming the glands, organs and bones of their prey. If your cat is fed a high-protein, varied diet it should receive all the vitamins and minerals necessary for its health – but you'd better check what is especially important, why and where to find it. It is only through informed selection that you can be sure that your cat is getting everything it needs, and from the very best sources.

SOME CAT FACTS

The B vitamins work in harmony within a complex group. Cats need a high and constant supply of them. They are all water soluble, and are usually found in the same foods, the most significant being brewer's yeast, liver, meat, poultry, game, fish, eggs and wholegrain cereals. Because they are water soluble they have to be replaced on a daily basis. Their value can be diminished and even destroyed if they are exposed to too much light, heat, oxidation, moisture or the presence of certain minerals.

Vitamins

Vitamins are organic substances that help regulate chemical reactions during the process of food-conversion into energy and body-building tissue. They also protect cells from toxins and infections. All mammals make extensive use of vitamins, and cats need them as much as we do.

Vitamins were only discovered during the twentieth century, and some may still be unknown. They have been given names corresponding to the letters of the alphabet, and are classified within two categories: those that are soluble in water (B and C), and those that are soluble in fat (A, D, E and K). The water-soluble vitamins have to be continually ingested, because if they are not immediately used they are washed out in the urine. The others, however, can be retained within body fat.

FAT-SOLUBLE VITAMINS

VITAMIN A

Source: animal tissue, liver, kidney, egg yolk, fish oils and butter.

Function: helps repair body tissue, promotes good eyesight and aids reproduction.

Deficiency: skin sores, problems with night vision and infertility. (An excess affects the bones, causing malformation and great pain).

VITAMIN D

Source: animal tissue, liver, egg yolk, fish oil, e.g., salmon, sardine, herring and mackerel; also naturally absorbed from sunshine.

Function: controls calcium/phosphorus balance and aids mineral transport to the bones and teeth.

Deficiency: weakness, brittle bones, spinal problems, muscle cramp, hardening of the arteries and malformed teeth.

VITAMIN E

Source: liver, egg yolk, wheat germ, wholegrain bread, oats and olive oil.

Function: acts as an antioxidant, aids reproduction and builds muscle.

Deficiency: muscle weakness, reproductive problems and steatitis – inflammation of body fat.

VITAMIN K

Source: egg yolk, yogurt, wholegrain cereals and oats.

Function: stimulates the production of substances involved in the normal blood-clotting process.

Deficiency: bleeding disorders – these are rare, because this vitamin can be manufactured by bacteria found in the intestines.

WATER-SOLUBLE VITAMINS

VITAMIN B1 (THIAMIN)

Source: brewer's yeast, wheatgerm, oats, liver and wholegrain cereals.

Function: necessary for the conversion of carbohydrates into energy and influences muscles, the nervous system and brain.

Deficiency: weakness, unsteadiness, nerve pain and numbness.

VITAMIN B2 (RIBOFLAVIN)

Source: liver, kidney, brewer's yeast, cooked fish, yogurt and cottage cheese.

Function: helps break down all food and is necessary both for good vision and cell respiration.

Deficiency: dermatitis, broken blood vessels and bloodshot eyes.

VITAMIN B3 (NIACIN)

Source: chicken liver, kidney, oily fish, bran, brewer's yeast, egg yolk and wheatgerm.

Function: assists metabolism and maintains the health of the skin, tongue and gums.

Deficiency: causes pellagra – whose symptoms include itching, an inflamed tongue, drooling and bad breath.

VITAMIN B5
(PANOTOTHENIC ACID)

Source: liver, kidney, bran, wheatgerm, brewer's yeast, dark-green vegetables and egg yolk.

Function: aids in the metabolism of energy and hormone production, and is also important in the manufacture of antibodies.

Deficiency: nervousness, irritability, proneness to infections and muscle-tingling.

VITAMIN B6 (PYRIDOXINE)

Source: brewer's yeast, liver, kidney, fish, egg yolk, wholegrain cereals, molasses and banana.

Function: essential in the breakdown of proteins and fats; aids in the formation of antibodies and is vital for red-blood-cell production.

Deficiency: slow development, muscular weakness, mouth disorders, anaemia and hair loss.

VITAMIN B9
(FOLIC ACID)

Source: liver, egg yolk, brewer's yeast and oysters.

Function: together with B12, it helps form red blood cells and influences the immune and nervous systems.

Deficiency: anaemia, weakness and weight loss.

VITAMIN B12
(CYANOCOBALAMIN)

Source: animal tissue, liver, kidney, fish, cheese and milk.

Function: necessary for the formation of red blood cells and the cellular function of the bone marrow and the nervous system.

Deficiency: general weakness and anaemia.

BIOTIN
(VITAMIN B COMPLEX)

Source: liver, kidney, egg yolk, brewer's yeast, oats and molasses.

Function: helps form fatty acids for the conversion of foods into energy.

Deficiency: fatigue, skin problems and hair loss.

CHOLINE
(VITAMIN B COMPLEX)

Source: fish, liver, wheatgerm and wholegrain cereals.

Function: aids in the breakdown and distribution of fats from the liver to cells and helps eliminate toxins.

Deficiency: liver disease and hardening of the arteries.

INOSITOL
(VITAMIN B COMPLEX)

Source: bran, oats, wheatgerm, brewer's yeast and molasses.

Function: together with choline helps keep the liver free of fats and toxins.

Deficiency: liver disease and poor appetite.

VITAMIN C
(ASCORBIC ACID)

Source: liver, kidney, dark-green vegetables, potatoes, sprouting greens, grass and most fruits.

Function: maintains the level of collagen, which is necessary for the formation of skin, ligaments and bones. Vital for healing, it also helps build up the immune system to protect against viruses.

Deficiency: slow healing, bleeding gums, susceptibility to infections, tendency to bruise or bleed. A prolonged deficiency may lead to scurvy.

Minerals

Minerals are inorganic substances that are found in the ground and the atmosphere; they are absorbed into animal tissue through food and breathing. They don't provide energy, but are essential for a host of metabolic processes, as well as the building of body parts – for example, calcium is vital for strong bones and teeth. They help the passage of chemical substances in and out of the cells, they control fluids – particularly the body's water balance – they build and maintain bones, they influence glands, muscle responses, nerve messages and immunity.

The most important are collectively known as macro-minerals – calcium, phosphorus, magnesium, potassium, sodium and chlorine – and your cat needs to ingest these every day. The others – trace minerals – are required only in minute amounts, but nevertheless have significant roles to play in maintaining the metabolism and overall health.

By checking the mineral chart you can work out the prime items that you should regularly include in your cat's diet in order to ensure an adequate supply of minerals. You should note, however, that most naturopathic veterinarians recommend feeding your cat a daily supplement.

MACRO-MINERALS

CALCIUM

Source: cheese, milk, yogurt, salmon, sardine, kelp, molasses and bone meal.

Function: builds and maintains bones and teeth in conjunction with vitamin D and the mineral phosphorus.

Deficiency: deterioration of bones, cramps and also rickets.

MAGNESIUM

Source: sardine, shrimp, wholegrain cereals, bone meal and molasses.

Function: important in cell metabolism, actuating more enzymes than any other mineral; it is essential for the absorption of sodium, potassium and calcium, and also for the complete use of the vitamins C, E and B complex.

Deficiency: poor bones, muscular weakness and heart and circulatory problems.

PHOSPHORUS

Source: animal meats, liver, fish, chicken, eggs, cheese, brewer's yeast and bone meal.

Function: the busiest of all minerals, it is found in every cell, and is involved in bone formation, as well as passing on hereditary genetic patterns.

Deficiency: poor-quality bones and teeth, low immunity and, in addition, reproduction difficulties.

POTASSIUM

Source: beef, chicken, wholegrain cereals, dark-green vegetables and bananas.

Function: often works in partnership with sodium, is important for the heart muscles, and also helps to regulate osmosis and the water balance.

Deficiency: muscular weakness, heart problems, dehydration and sluggish kidneys.

SODIUM AND CHLORINE

Source: animal tissue, chicken, kelp, seafood and salt.

Function: together with potassium, they balance the water content of the body, as well as the acid-alkali levels, and influence blood pressure.

Deficiency: water-retention problems, muscular cramps; an excess raises blood pressure and swells body tissue.

TRACE MINERALS

CHROMIUM

Source: brewer's yeast, molasses and also shellfish.

Function: helps regulate blood-sugar levels and improves the body's utilisation of glucose.

Deficiency: high blood sugar and hardening of the arteries.

COBALT

Source: liver, kidney, eggs and cheese.

Function: necessary for the proper functioning of vitamin B12 and also the red blood cells.

Deficiency: fatigue and anaemia.

COPPER

Source: liver, kidney, shellfish and also wheatgerm.

Function: associated with the iron production of the red blood cells; important for hair pigment; and a catalyst for the body-building enzymes connected with muscle and nerve fibres and collagen production.

Deficiency: anaemia and healing problems.

IODINE

Source: fish, poultry and kelp.

Function: needed for the production of the thyroid hormone.

Deficiency: abnormal swelling in the throat leading to a goitre, weight gain, lethargy and hair loss.

IRON

Source: red meat, liver, kidney, egg yolk and also molasses.

Function: transports oxygen to the red blood cells and muscles; it is most beneficial when also in the presence of vitamin C.

Deficiency: anaemia, fatigue and limited growth.

MANGANESE

Source: wholegrain cereals, egg yolk and also wheatgerm.

Function: helps form bone and soft tissues; important for the maintenance of reproductive processes.

Deficiency: bad co-ordination, sterility and also birth defects.

SELENIUM

Source: liver, kidney, fish and also wholegrain cereals.

Function: closely associated with vitamin E; acts as an antioxidant and contributes to muscle development.

Deficiency: limited utilisation of vitamin E; an excess causes brittle bones, tooth decay and hair loss.

SULPHUR

Source: animal tissue, cheese and eggs.

Function: helps in the formation of all body tissues, and is necessary for the proper function of the vitamins thiamin and biotin.

Deficiency: impeded growth and development.

ZINC

Source: muscle meats, liver, egg yolk, shellfish, wheatgerm, brewer's yeast and garlic.

Function: influences the immune system and sexual development, and plays a part in the condition of skin and hair.

Deficiency: delayed sexual maturity, retarded growth and hair loss.

If left unsupervised for too long, your cat will almost certainly slip its paw into a cocktail dip in preference to its health-food formula.

SOME CAT FACTS

Not all cats can cope with milk. It's not so much that they don't like it, but more because it doesn't agree with the cat's digestive system. It is the lactose (sugar) in cow's milk that's the enemy. However, cats can tolerate goat's or sheep's milk, which is in any case better for them. Natural yogurt is also well tolerated – cats like it and it is of special nutritional value.

THE BIG FORTIFIER: THE DAILY SUPPLEMENT

With all this fresh food now being fed to your cat, you may think that you've done your bit and that it's up to your pet to come up with rewarding results in the form of improved shape and fitness. However, there's just one more thing: a concentrated supplement of the most significant vitamins and minerals.

Is this really necessary? In theory it shouldn't be, but in modern times the cat's need for vitamins and minerals has increased dramatically because of the reduced quality of even fresh foods, the pollution in the air and in the ground. Stress, too, plays a part, because the noise and pace of urban living also affects the cat's nervous system.

Holistic veterinarians are united in their belief that regular additions of certain vitamins and minerals contained within natural sources to a cat's diet do it the power of good. Here is a selection of their recommended formulas.

Suggested formulas

Richard H Pitcairn, the American doyen of natural health care for animals, suggests two daily supplements in his book *Natural health for dogs and cats*: a cat-powder mix and a cat-oil mix, a teaspoon of each to be fed daily, plus 30–50 IU of vitamin E (from capsules) as a prime oxidant and protector of the essential vitamin A. The ingredients can be found in most health-food shops.

Cat-powder-mix formula

½ cup brewer's yeast
¼ cup bone meal (powdered form for human use)
¼ cup kelp powder

Mix the ingredients together very well and store in a sealed jar on a dark shelf.

Cat-oil-mix formula

¾ cup olive oil
¼ cup cod-liver oil
20–40 IU vitamin E
  (to prevent spoilage)

Shake the ingredients
together in a sealed
brown bottle and
store in the refrigerator.

If your cat is canny and questions the addition of supplements to its food, you could try rubbing a little on its paw, which it will then happily lick off.

Juliette de Baïracli Levy, the renowned naturalist and author of *Cats naturally*, comes up with this daily tonic: to a tablespoon of powdered seaweed add one teaspoon of mixed, finely chopped or minced leaves (choose from parsley, chickweed, fennel or dill, clover, dandelion, nasturtium, cress or mint). Include as much variety as possible. Mix well and sprinkle a tablespoon into the cat's food daily.

Edmund R Dorosz, a Canadian veterinarian, details in his book *Let's cook for our cat* his plans for both a dry and liquid supplement.

DRY SUPPLEMENT

1 cup brewer's yeast
1 cup bone meal
1 cup sunflower seeds, ground fine
½ cup sodium ascorbate
¼ cup kelp
2 tablespoons catnip (for smell and taste)

Mix the ingredients together and store in an airtight container in the refrigerator. The daily dosage is 1 teaspoon daily for adults; 1½ teaspoons for queens with kittens; and ½ teaspoon for kittens.

LIQUID SUPPLEMENT

½ cup cod-liver oil
¼ cup wheatgerm oil
1 tablespoon garlic oil

Mix and shake the ingredients in an airtight, dark container and store in the dark. The daily dosage is ½ to 1 teaspoon for medium-sized cats; up to 1 tablespoon for large, active and pregnant cats; and ¼ teaspoon for kittens.

Anitra Frazier, in her book *The new natural cat*, gives her own version of a vitamin-mineral supplement, and once a week also squeezes the contents of one 400-unit vitamin-E capsule into the cat's food. She also offers a very sensible suggestion: rub the vitamin-E oil onto the cat's paw and it will happily lick it off.

VITA-MINERAL MIX

1½ cup brewer's yeast
¼ cup kelp powder
1 cup lethicin granules
2 cups wheat bran
2 cups bone meal

Mix the ingredients together and store in a covered container in the refrigerator. Give the cat 2 teaspoonfuls per day, spread throughout the meals.

You will probably have noticed that there are many ingredients common to these formulas, which are clearly considered prime nutrients by most naturopathic veterinarians.

The problem is that your cat may not be in complete agreement with such all-inclusive offerings when it comes to their palatability, particularly in the case of the oils. You can actually work out your own, optimal mix, using one element at a time, adding and subtracting ingredients until you come up with something that meets the dual demands of your nutritional knowledge and your cat's taste. The amounts given in the box opposite are a dosage guide, as suggested by veterinarian Edmund R Dorosz.

(A word of warning: you can go overboard with some vitamins, in particular the fat-soluble vitamins A and D, which can be stored in body fat and may become toxic. There are also inherent dangers in excessive doses of calcium and phosphorus.)

If you can convince a mother cat that the vita-mineral mix is an appetising addition to her diet, her kittens will soon follow her example.

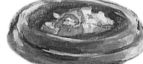

The egg situation: eggs are a fine source of protein, but the egg white must never be served raw because it contains a chemical which destroys essential B-group vitamins. Egg yolks can be stirred raw into food. If cooked, the whole egg is best scrambled, but an egg meal should not be served more than twice a week.

CHANGING TO HOME-MADE MEALS: EASY DOES IT

The only effective method in changing your stubborn cat's diet to a natural, home-made one is gradually to reduce the quantity of its usual food, topping up the amount with fresh produce and mixing it together with a sprinkling of a vitamin-and-mineral supplement. Your cat needs time to get used to the smell and taste of the new foods and its digestive system must have the chance to adjust.

The cat's body has to go through a natural cleansing process, and a too abrupt change of diet can give its metabolism quite a shock. Possible side effects may include diarrhoea, strong-smelling urine and blooded faeces. This transitional process will take between two and three weeks, and at the beginning you may very well have a complete strike on your hands – a refusal to eat anything. Don't panic, your cat's just seeing if it can get away with it.

The super elixirs

BREWER'S YEAST (VITAMIN B COMPLEX):
1 teaspoon daily; all ages

BONE MEAL (CALCIUM AND PHOSPHORUS):
¼ teaspoon daily; all ages

KELP/SEAWEED (IODINE AND MINERALS):
¼ teaspoon daily; all ages

COD-LIVER OIL (VITAMINS A AND D):
1 teaspoon weekly for adults;
½ teaspoon per week for kittens

WHEATGERM OIL (VITAMIN E):
1 teaspoon over 3 days for adults;
1 teaspoon over 5 days for kittens

6 Cooking for your cat

Cooking for your cat is no big deal. Firstly, your cat doesn't care about presentation, so you can happily throw all the ingredients together anyhow, which eliminates one of the main pressures of cooking. Cats do, however, care about smell, taste, texture and freshness. What you have to care about is the quality and nutritional balance of the foods that you feed your cat and the ways in which you prepare them. This is actually quite easy, and can all be done with a minimum of fuss. All cooked dishes can be stored or refrigerated for future use – no one wants to be fiddling around preparing minute portions all the time.

Don't expect your cat to run around in circles at the sheer pleasure of being served a new dish. Cats aren't like that: they're inherently suspicious, and like you to know it. And, of course, not all cats like everything. Home-cooking for cats is very much a trial-and-error procedure.

I've been experimenting with feline cuisine for many years, and it never ceases to amaze me how one cat will lap up everything while another – even a close relative of the enthusiast – will turn up its nose at your offering in what seems very much like disgust. Cats will quickly let you know what they fancy, and together you can work out an acceptable regular menu meeting your dual demands.

It's important to make your cat's diet varied. Don't permit your cat to cajole you into feeding it just one or two favoured dishes. I usually have a standard repertoire of five, with additional, nourishing snacks always at hand. I alternate these with whatever suitable fresh food is left over from the family table – bits of roast meat or poultry, fish, and so on, which have all been cooked perfectly plainly. The remains of certain family meals can actually be recycled into a worthy dish for your cat by adding a few ingredients that are relevant to the cat's particular needs. For example, the carcass of a roast chicken can become a delicious cat's chicken mould.

And the cost of cooking for your cat? This depends on how clever you are at buying ingredients, but home-cooked meals are certainly cheaper than those at the upper end of the commercial pet-food market, and are on a par with the average. However, there's no comparison when it comes to nutritional value. Furthermore, if you manage to combine the ingredients of your family meals with the special requirements of the cat, the extra amount all but disappears into the household budget.

The odd thing is that cats seem to understand what's going on when you're cooking good food for them. Well, I like to think so anyway, no matter how sceptical professional cat behaviourists may be. There's not only a lot of swishing going on around the legs when I'm cooking, but also a fair amount of patient sitting, with the cats' eyes and noses clearly keeping track of what is happening. But then I do talk to my cats and discuss the menu with them, which may sound silly to some, but I really think that cats enjoy it. After all, it is a form of constructive togetherness, and also promotes your cat's fitness by keeping it awake, alert and conscious of your tender loving care.

The good ingredients

MEAT, POULTRY AND GAME:
beef, lamb, chicken, turkey, duck, venison, rabbit, quail, pheasant, guinea fowl, pigeon; also liver, kidney and tongue

FISH:
all types of fresh or canned salmon, mackerel, sardine and tuna

DAIRY AND FARMYARD PRODUCE:
milk (preferably goat's), butter, soft, white cheeses, Parmesan, yogurt and eggs (primarily the yolks)

GRAINS:
oats, maize, brown rice, pasta and wholegrain breads

VEGETABLES:
carrots, courgettes (zucchini), green-leaf brassicas, garlic and parsley

The cat's kitchen cupboard

Although you need to think mostly in terms of buying fresh food, there are certain staples that are invaluable and should be at hand for whipping up snacks, as well as for preparing planned or emergency meals.

STAPLE FOODS

Dried: oats, oatmeal, rice, pasta, wholemeal flour and bouillon cubes

Canned: salmon, mackerel, sardine, tuna and soft cod roes

Bottled: cockles and mussels

Frozen: chicken livers, shrimps, fish, ground meat and poultry

Liquid: extra-virgin olive oil, cold pressed

Herbs: garlic, thyme and iodised salt

Your cat likes to keep up with what's going on in the kitchen; it's also an excellent way of spending quality time together.

SMART COOKING

There is little point in buying the very best ingredients and then destroying many of the valuable nutrients that they contain during cooking. Over-cooking is the main culprit in this respect, as is boiling in water. The reason for this is because heat can alter the composition of the essential amino acids in proteins, while the water-soluble vitamins (B complex and C) can literally dissolve and be washed away unless the liquid is preserved – as in a broth – and put to good use in a recipe. In cat cuisine most nutrients need minimal cooking, and many none at all. Here's a guide to cooking ingredients correctly.

PLANNING MEALS

It is perfectly easy to present your cat with great meals without going to the extent of following specific recipes, although these are useful when preparing nutritious snacks. If you follow the guide in the 'Getting the diet right' chapter (pages 64–89), feline dishes can be compiled from fresh produce very simply. Just mix the ingredients together, making sure that the protein ratio is between 35 and 45 per cent, the fat ratio is between 20 and 35 per cent, and that the remaining carbohydrate balance involves either a mix or

some fresh vegetables and some starchy fibre.

The addition of a daily vitamin/mineral supplement will further help to ensure that all the essentials are contained in a meal. But don't get paranoid about so-called 'completeness' in either a single meal or in your cat's daily diet. Satisfying your cat's nutritional needs can be spread over many days and, if you throw something inadequate into the bowl one day, there should be no cause for guilt, as no doubt it will be compensated for over the succeeding days. Cats can – and have – survived on meagre nutrients for years. They do, after all, have nine lives!

Remember that cats like moist food, served at room temperature. So if any suitable left-overs look a bit dry, or if a prepared dish is cold from the refrigerator, the right consistency and heat can always be achieved by adding a luke-warm broth made from prepared stock or, at a pinch, a bouillon cube or can of consommé (this is wicked, I know, and it must be well diluted because of its high sodium/salt content). This method also helps fool your cat into believing that the food has been freshly prepared for it, and that it is therefore especially appetising.

In an emergency, commercial dry and canned food can be incorporated into whatever natural ingredients are available – some

From the health-food store

The following items make very useful additions to home-made meals and can often be incorporated into recipes. Some can be mixed into a daily vitamin/mineral supplement.

SUPPLEMENTS

Bone meal: for calcium and phosphorus

Brewer's yeast: for essential B-group vitamins

Bran: for fibre and thiamine

Cod-liver oil: for vitamins A and D

Kelp powder: for minerals, especially iodine

Vitamin E: for concentrated doses of the vitamin obtained from capsules

Wheatgerm: for vitamin E

Cooking techniques

MEATS AND POULTRY:

these are best roasted on the bone, but not for long; beef and lamb can be pink, poultry just to the point of turning. A good idea is to wrap the meat in foil to preserve its juices; boiling works in a restricted liquid stew. All meat and poultry must be completely boned before serving; cut into small pieces.

FISH:

never fry fish; the most nutritious method is to wrap it in foil and bake it in the oven for 10 to 15 minutes, less for a small fish. Steaming is also acceptable; boiling will destroy nutrients. Be very meticulous about removing all the bones.

GRAINS:

grains have to be cooked in the same way as we cook them for ourselves: boiled in water until thoroughly soft, as cats cannot easily metabolise starchy carbohydrates.

VEGETABLES:

if vegetables are grated or chopped very finely they are most beneficial when eaten raw; otherwise steam or lightly boil them, but always cut them up into almost indiscernible pieces to mimic how these botanicals would be naturally found in the prey's stomach.

SEASONINGS:

seasonings are mostly unappreciated, but salt is recognised to a degree, so it's a good idea to add a little, the best being iodised salt as this will introduce useful iodine to the body. Otherwise just use garlic — for health, not taste — and thyme every now and then as an antioxidant, while vitamin-packed brewer's yeast furthermore adds flavour to every meal.

of the following recipes give examples of this. With practice you'll become instinctively aware of what needs to be added – and so will your cat, who'll be the first to let you know if something is amiss.

MEASUREMENT GUIDE

What makes cooking for cats a so much more relaxed procedure than cooking for ourselves is that including exact weights of ingredients is not of dire importance. A dish is not going to be ruined if you add too much or too little, nor are you concerned with subtleties of taste, but rather with the balance of nutrients. So a bit more here or a bit less there doesn't matter, provided that it remains within the suggested range of protein/fat/carbohydrate proportions. Most of the measurements in the recipes that follow are given in terms of spoons and cups, which we all have to hand.

When weights are given, these should be considered as being in any case approximate; and you should not worry too much when converting grams to ounces, or *vice versa*.

WEIGHT MAINTENANCE

The natural diet explained in the following pages will not only maintain your cat's optimum health, but will also keep its weight stable. This is because all the meals that are included are highly nutritious and contain no surplus junk, and cats have furthermore shown their ability to control their calorie intake on this regimen. They are satisfied with reasonable portions – two to three tablespoons, two or three times within a twenty-four-hour period – and don't keep going back for more, even if additional food is offered or left around.

WEIGHT LOSS

If you are trying to help your cat to lose weight, the same foods should be used in the recommended proportions, but the portions should be smaller: one to two tablespoons given more frequently – four or five times a day. Feeding should be a stretched-out process involving a slow reduction from high to low quantities of food. When your cat's weight goal has been achieved, you can gradually build up the amount of food that you feed it to the level of maintenance portions.

Recipes

Fortified stocks, gravies and sauces

Fortified stocks, gravies and sauces are the most useful and fundamental contributors to healthy cat cookery. Bones and pieces of protein-packed meat, poultry, game and fish can be boiled together with vegetables and vitamin/mineral supplements to make the most nutritious addition to any dish. They can be mixed with commercial products, used to turn our left-overs into valuable cat meals, and can form a major ingredient of recipes. House-bound cats rarely enjoy a fresh bone, but they can reap the benefits of its mineral content indirectly – if not to such a high degree – by eating the following stock recipes. Don't throw away any bones – even from a chop or a chicken wing – for they can all be flung in your cat's stockpot. As for fresh bones: a family butcher will always have a supply available at a very reasonable cost – indeed, probably for nothing if you buy other things. Stocks can be stored in the refrigerator, but a week is about the limit.

Cats rarely get the benefit of a good bone but if one is served, it should be of a manageable size.

MIXED-MEAT STOCK

2 lb (1 kg) mixed raw bones, knuckles
and, if around, any left-over roast
meat on the bone
3 carrots, sliced
4 garlic cloves
2 stalks celery
1 teaspoon iodised salt
1 tablespoon olive oil
1 tablespoon brewer's yeast
1 tablespoon bone meal
2 tablespoons cod-liver oil
1 teaspoon dried thyme

This can be made with a combination of raw and cooked bones of beef, lamb or veal, but not pork. It can moisten dishes as it is, or can be thickened into a sauce by adding the liquid to a roux made from butter and wholemeal flour.

Brown the bones in the olive oil. Add garlic, carrots, celery, thyme and iodised salt. Pour in water to cover the bones and bring to the boil; reduce heat, cover and simmer for a couple of hours. Skim off any fat that appears during cooking. Strain. Cool to a luke-warm state, then stir in the brewer's yeast, bone meal and cod-liver oil. Refrigerate in a sealed jar.

MIXED-POULTRY STOCK

The basic meat-stock recipe above can be followed, substituting any mixture of poultry and game in the place of the meat. Even a simple chicken stock is of great value. Poultry often produces more jelly, so if the stock is cooked for longer and greatly reduced, the more solidified end product can be equally well combined with both fresh and processed foods.

FISH STOCK

2 lb (1 kg) fish bones,
heads, pieces and left-overs
3 cloves garlic
2 stalks celery
2 sliced carrots
1 teaspoon thyme
2 tablespoons chopped parsley
½ teaspoon iodised salt
1 tablespoon brewer's yeast
1 tablespoon bone meal
2 tablespoons cod-liver oil

The best fish stock is made from all the things lying on the fishmonger's floor, namely the heads and skeletons that are left after filleting. There is usually an abundance of these, and you can get them for little cost. Needless to say, they look awful – but wash well. Any bits from all varieties of fish can also go in the pot, including shellfish.

Put the fish, vegetables, herbs and salt into a deep pan, cover with water and bring to the boil; reduce heat and simmer for about an hour. Strain, cool, then stir in the brewer's yeast, bone meal and cod-liver oil. Refrigerate in a sealed jar.

Snacks and treats

Snacks and treats are normally frowned upon in any animal diet plan, but that is because the commercial ones are invariably full of preservatives and additives and are disturbingly lacking in nutrients. But cats adore little extras, and there is no reason why these should be banned if they are good and wholesome. In fact, they are very useful in a slimming regimen, as they can regarded as one of the 'small meals' recommended four or six times a day – they are that nutritious. And your cat will smugly think that it's managed to wangle a special treat. It is better still to feed them as a reward for a bit of exertion, such as chasing a ball or jumping through a hoop. In this way exercise plus snack equals fitness. Your cat will thus believe that it's really accomplished something, and will be keener to do the muscle-working trick again.

Cats need their rest, but you must be vigilant in seeing that they don't exceed the norm of sixteen hours a day.

MEAT-AND-WHEAT SNACKS

¾ cup boiling water
1 bouillon cube (chicken or meat)
2 tablespoons ground beef, lamb
or chicken
4 cups wholewheat flour
2 tablespoons wheatgerm
1 oz butter
2 cloves garlic, crushed
2 tablespoons molasses or black treacle
1 teaspoon bone meal

These can be made in quantity and stored in airtight jars. All my cats have leapt upon them, as they are crunchy and obviously taste good. Butter may seem extravagant, but it's only a little and should never be replaced by margarine. Although cats don't easily register sweet tastes, the molasses provide many important minerals, as well as texture.

Pre-heat the oven to 180°C/350°F/gas-mark 4. Dissolve the bouillon cube in boiling water. In a separate bowl, mix the ground meat, flour, wheatgerm, bone meal and garlic; add the butter, integrating it with your fingers. Stir in the molasses or black treacle and then the bouillon liquid. Knead to form a firm paste. Roll out to a thickness of approximately 1¼ inch. Cut into squares and place on a greased baking tray. Bake for 20 minutes, then turn over and bake for a further 15 minutes. Leave to cool. Store in a jar and break into small pieces before serving.

OATS-AND-MEAT FLAPJACKS

4 oz (100 g) ground beef, chicken
or turkey
4 oz (100 g) wholewheat flour
4 oz (100 g) rolled oats
4 oz (100 g) butter
2 tablespoons molasses or black treacle
1 tablespoon brewer's yeast
50 mg taurine (from a capsule)
1 teaspoon ground almonds (optional)

I discovered that my cats loved flapjacks, so here is a kitty-cat version which provides a high level of protein in the meat and oats, as well as balanced nutrients in the other ingredients, but which eliminates the lethal sugar that is contained in the human version.

Pre-heat the oven to 180°C/350°F/gas-mark 4. Cream together the butter and molasses or black treacle. Stir in the wholewheat flour, rolled oats, brewer's yeast, taurine and ground almonds; finally add the ground meat. Add a little water if the consistency is too dry. Knead the mixture into a ball and roll out on a floured surface. Cut into squares and place on a lightly greased baking sheet. Bake for 10 to 15 minutes. Cool and then store in jars, breaking into small pieces when served.

Savoury spreads and pâtés

It may come as a surprise to learn that cats absolutely love savoury spreads and pâtés, though on second thoughts it's a rare cat that hasn't managed to get its paws into your cocktail dips or on human snacks at one time or another. Cats like them because so many are fishy and creamy. Why not let your cat have its own platter? These bits and pieces register very highly on the healthy-eating scale.

It's a good idea to have a selection of healthy, home-made spreads to hand. These can be stored in little pots and kept safely in the refrigerator for quite a while. I spread them on toasted, wholegrain bread, which provides the appreciated crunch factor as well as extra nutrients. I may even go so far as to spread a little butter on first. The toast should be cut into small squares.

If this two-layered dish is a new culinary concept to your cat, it will doubtless lick off the tasty top first, but because a certain amount of the spread will have been absorbed into the toast, it won't be long before your newly attuned gourmet will get around to eating the more solid, filling bits. Such a titbit may be a meal in itself if necessary.

SMOKED-HADDOCK PÂTÉ

1 piece of smoked haddock
Butter
1 teaspoon brewer's yeast
½ teaspoon fresh parsley, finely chopped

Pour boiling water over the fish, cover and leave for 10 minutes; skin and flake it. Cover and weight it to pull out the excess water. Mash with enough butter to make a spreadable purée. Add the brewer's yeast and parsley. Mash again and put in a small covered container. Refrigerate.

KIPPER PÂTÉ

Do exactly the same as for the haddock paste, but be sure to take out all the bones first.

SARDINE SPREAD

1 can sardines in vegetable or olive oil (not tomato sauce)
Butter
½ teaspoon brewer's yeast or kelp powder
½ teaspoon raw carrot, finely grated
½ teaspoon fresh parsley, minced

Open the can of sardines and drain off the oil. Bone the sardines. Mash with enough butter to make a spreadable paste. Add the brewer's yeast or kelp powder, as well as the carrot and parsley. Mash well and refrigerate in a covered container.

COD'S-ROE PÂTÉ (HOME-MADE TARAMASALATA)

1 medium-sized potato
1 clove of garlic, crushed
1 can cod's roe
Olive oil
Pinch of thyme

Boil the potato in unsalted water. Cool and mash. Open the can of cod's roe and drain off any excess liquid. Mash the roe with the garlic, adding as much olive oil as is necessary to make a creamy, quite fluid, mixture. Then stir in the mashed potato, adding the thyme. Pack into little jars and refrigerate.

CHICKEN-LIVER MOUSSE

8 oz (250 g) chicken livers
4 oz (100 g) butter
1 clove garlic, crushed
Pinch of thyme

Clean the livers thoroughly, removing the bile bag and filaments. Sauté in a little hot butter until they just change colour. Add the garlic and thyme and cook for only a few more minutes – the insides must remain pink. Bring to a paste in a blender with the rest of the butter. Put into small pots and seal with a layer of melted butter.

KIPPER MOUSSE

1 fat kipper
Butter
2 tablespoons cream or yogurt

Poach the kipper in boiling water for about 5 minutes. Bone and cool. Mash with enough butter to make a smooth paste. Add a couple of tablespoons of cream or yogurt and bring to a spreading consistency in the blender. Your eye has to judge how much cream or yogurt needs to be added.

Sandwiches

Believe or not, cats like sandwiches – provided, of course, that they are cut into appetising and easily edible squares, and have a smear of butter and a delicious filling. It's like tea at the Ritz for cats, and who's going to turn their nose up at that? The bread has to be crunchy, chunky and wholegrain – the fresher, the better. Any of the savouries previously listed can be put into a sandwich, but here are a few other tasty suggestions.

The nutritious fillings

SARDINES:
bone and mash with a small pot of cream cheese or cottage cheese; add a teaspoon of finely chopped parsley

SALMON:
bone and mash with a teaspoon of freshly grated carrot and half a teaspoon of brewer's yeast

SHRIMPS:
mix potted shrimps with a little cottage cheese and any available fresh greens, grated

HADDOCK:
flaked, smoked haddock, cooked and mixed with a little cream and finely chopped parsley

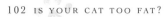

Eggs

Eggs provide a powerhouse of nutrients for cats, but only the yolk can be used raw – on average three a week can be mixed into any meal. The whole egg must be cooked, and if you add a few ingredients that smell and taste good, your cat will eagerly eat everything up.

CRUNCHY SCRAMBLED EGGS

1 egg
1 dessertspoon cold water
1 teaspoon butter
1 teaspoon very finely chopped parsley or any leaf greens
Handful of commercial dried cat food

These are perfect for an emergency meal. All you need is an egg, some dried commercial cat food and any fresh greens.

Beat the egg and add the water (don't think of using milk). Melt the butter in a small pan over a low heat, pour in the egg and whisk it with a fork until it scrambles. Take off the heat and stir in the greens and dried food.

SCRAMBLED EGGS WITH HADDOCK

4 oz (100 g) smoked haddock
¼ cup milk
2 eggs
1 dessertspoon cream or yogurt
2 teaspoons butter
1 dessertspoon finely chopped parsley

This is a rather more ambitious recipe than the other scrambled-egg dish. It can be made with any fish, but, like us, cats recognise the special appeal of smoked haddock. Not all cats can tolerate cream, so yogurt can be used as an alternative. This recipe makes enough for two portions.

Poach the haddock in the milk for about 5 minutes. Drain and flake, taking out any lurking bones. Whisk the eggs. Put a little of the butter into a pan, pour in the beaten eggs and stir until they start to thicken. Add the fish and the rest of the butter; continue to stir off the heat. Add the cream or yogurt and parsley.

SLIMMER'S OMELETTE

⅓ tablespoon non-fat dry milk
1 medium egg
1 tablespoon dry-curd cottage cheese
½ tablespoon finely chopped or grated vegetables

Richard H Pitcairn suggests this weight-loss dish in his book *Natural health for dogs and cats*, and recommends that it be taken with his daily vitamin/mineral supplement (see page 88).

Mix the dry milk with a little water and beat with the egg. Put a small dab of butter into a skillet, heat well and pour in the egg mixture. When cooked on one side, turn over and place the cottage cheese and vegetables on top. Allow to cook a little and fold over. Serve in small pieces.

SAVOURY CAT CRÊPES

I accidentally discovered that cats like pancakes, and realised that it was an easy way in which to introduce protein to a cat's diet from several good sources, and also to sneak in supplements. The crêpes can be made in bulk, refrigerated, reheated and filled when needed.

BASIC BATTER RECIPE
5 oz (125 g) wholemeal flour
1 teaspoon bone meal
1 cup milk
Pinch iodised salt
1 dessertspoon olive oil
½ pint water
2 eggs

Mix the milk and water and gradually add to the flour and bone meal, beating constantly so that the batter becomes as smooth as it can be when you are using wholemeal flour. Break in the eggs, add the salt and oil. Beat the batter until smooth, adjusting the consistency with water if necessary; it should be quite thin. Set aside to rest for an hour or two.

Heat a frying pan and grease it very slightly with butter. Wait until the pan is very hot, pour in about ¼ cup of the batter and move it around until the surface is covered. Cook very quickly; turn over. Pile up the crêpes using grease-proof paper dividers. They can actually be frozen, but require 2 to 3 hours to thaw out.

CREAMED SHRIMP:
quickly cook 1 tablespoon chopped shrimp in a little butter, add a dessertspoon cream or yogurt, plus 1 teaspoon finely chopped parsley.

CHICKEN LIVERS AND CHEESE:
lightly cook in a little butter 1 tablespoon finely chopped liver, 1 tablespoon cottage cheese, 1 teaspoon grated carrot and 1 teaspoon finely chopped greens.

RUSSIAN TREAT:
combine 1 tablespoon chopped herring or smoked salmon with 1 teaspoon each of caviar and sour cream; add ½ teaspoon finely chopped parsley.

Game

Cats love game, probably because of the slightly wild smell that it has. The lean flesh is a concentrated source of protein. All types of game can be roasted or baked in the oven, but be careful not to over-cook it, otherwise the meat can become very dry – and cats like their food to have a high water content. Allow the flesh just to turn colour. A good way to preserve its moisture is to wrap the game in foil.

MALTESE RABBIT PIE

1 tablespoon olive oil

3 cloves garlic, crushed

1 lb (500 g) boneless rabbit portions, cut into cubes

1 tablespoon flour

1 tablespoon bone meal

1 cup chicken stock (best home-made, but can be prepared using a stock cube)

1 teaspoon thyme

1 dessertspoon finely chopped parsley

½ teaspoon iodised salt

4 tablespoons potatoes, mashed using butter and milk

I once spent some time in Malta, which has a high feral-cat population and boasts rabbit as its national dish. I used to treat the feline rovers who stalked into my garden to this dish; needless to say, not a scrap was ever left.

Pre-heat oven to 180°C/350°F/gas-mark 4. Mix the flour, bone meal and iodised salt and toss in the rabbit pieces and coat them. Heat the oil in a skillet, add the garlic and cook for a minute; shake the excess flour off the rabbit and brown all over. Remove to an oven-proof dish. Stir any remaining flour into the pan juices and cook for a minute, then stir in the stock gradually and bring to the boil. Add the thyme and parsley. Stir well. Pour the sauce over the rabbit. Cover with a lid or foil and cook for 1 hour. Top with the mashed potatoes and quickly brown to a crisp under the grill.

Cats are drawn to the slightly wild smell of game.

VENISON STEW

1 tablespoon olive oil
1 lb (500 g) venison cubes
(don't trim the fat)
1 carrot, finely diced
2 sticks celery, complete with leaves
3 cloves garlic, crushed
1 tablespoon flour
1 tablespoon bone meal
½ teaspoon iodised salt
1 cup chicken stock
(home-made or from a cube)
1 teaspoon thyme
1 teaspoon finely chopped parsley

I've found that my cats like the chewiness of venison, for it demands more masticatory effort than other meats. Be careful not to cut the pieces too small, as cats are inclined to swallow them whole. This dish keeps well and can be served with rice, chopped pasta or mashed potatoes.

Heat the oil in a heavy saucepan and brown the venison cubes over a high heat; remove. Put the carrot and garlic in the pan and cook for a minute. Stir in the flour and bone meal, cooking for a few minutes; gradually blend in the stock and bring to the boil, always stirring. Add the venison, salt, celery sticks and thyme. Mix in well. Lower the heat, cover and simmer for 1 hour. When cooked, remove the celery sticks and discard; stir in the parsley.

PIGEON OR QUAIL WITH OATMEAL STUFFING

OATMEAL STUFFING
¼ lb (100 g) rolled oats
1 tablespoon bone meal
2 garlic cloves, crushed
2 tablespoons finely chopped parsley
½ teaspoon iodised salt
1 egg
2 tablespoons milk
1 dessertspoon finely chopped parsley
1 dessertspoon grated carrot
1 dessertspoon finely chopped greens
(any variety)

COOKING THE BIRD
1 pigeon or quail
1 tablespoon olive oil

Your cat won't appreciate the visual appeal of this dish, of course, but the stuffing represents good nutritional value and also absorbs the bird's juices whilst cooking. Unfortunately, you cannot serve it straight from the oven, but you could show it to your cat before carving and boning it – and every bone must be removed, which means that this initially rather aesthetically pleasing meal ends up looking a mess. But oh, how tasty!

To make the stuffing, beat the egg with the milk. Mix together all the other ingredients and bind them with the liquid. If too dry, moisten with a little water.

The method is the same for both pigeon and quail – only the cooking time varies. Heat 1 tablespoon of olive oil in a pan and brown the bird all over at a high heat. Remove. If any juices are left in the pan, add them to the stuffing. Stuff the bird, wrap it in foil and place in a roasting pan. Set the oven temperature at 160°C/325°F/gas-mark 3. Cook the pigeon for 1½ hours or the quail for 40 minutes.

Meat

All meats provide body-building protein and essential amino acids. It's easy enough to cook them in straightforward ways, but many recipes can incorporate the vital vitamins and minerals which otherwise would have to be added as a supplement. Some dishes have the great advantage that they can to be safely preserved in the refrigerator, needing only a few minutes to warm up.

BAKED MEAT LOAF

1 cup brown rice
2 cups chicken broth
(can be made from
a cube or granules)
1 lb (500 g) ground meat
(you could substitute
chicken or turkey)
1 cup mixed green and
orange/yellow vegetables,
cooked or raw,
finely chopped or grated
1 teaspoon olive oil
1 garlic clove, minced
50 mg taurine

A few years ago, when I was in California, I opened the *Los Angeles Times* and found – much to my delight and astonishment – a whole page devoted to home-cooking for pets: dogs, cats and parrots. It was cleverly headed 'It's dining cats and dogs'. The following recipe devised by Hollywood veterinarian Dr John Limehouse was featured, which I promptly made. It worked out very well, though when serving slices after storage I found that my cats were happier if I added a moisturising stock or gravy – if you have none to hand, make a little from boiling water and half a bouillon cube.

Cook the brown rice in the chicken broth until the liquid is totally absorbed – about 20 minutes. Remove from heat and add the ground meat or poultry, vegetables, oil, garlic and taurine. Pre-heat the oven to 180°C/350°F/gas-mark 4. Pack the mixture into a greased loaf tin and bake for 1 hour. Leave to cool. Divide into 10 portions and store in the refrigerator or freezer. Serve at room temperature.

KIDNEYS SAUTÉ

½ lb (500 g) lamb or veal kidneys
1 dessertspoon butter
½ teaspoon iodised salt
1 clove crushed garlic
1 teaspoon kelp
1 tablespoon bone meal
1 dessertspoon finely chopped parsley

This is a very quick dish, full of goodness. Use lamb or veal kidneys, because others can be very strong and may contain unhealthy amounts of urine. Most cats like kidneys – and the protective fat is also beneficial, so don't cut it away. Serve mixed with rice, pasta or rolled oats.

Skin the kidneys, retain the cores and slice them finely, then quarter the slices. In a heavy skillet, heat the butter, add the garlic, then the kidneys, salt and kelp; sauté slowly, stirring all the time. At the last minute, stir in the bone meal and parsley.

COTSWOLDS-CAT LAMB CASSEROLE

1 dessertspoon olive oil
6 oz (150 g) cubed lamb (frozen)
½ onion, finely chopped
½ carrot, finely diced
½ teaspoon thyme
¾ pint beef stock (made from a cube)
1 tablespoon flour
1 tablespoon bone meal
50 mg taurine

Rebecca Wardle lives in the English countryside and, although she's only nine years old, insists on cooking for her cats, despite the fact that they probably do quite a bit of hunting. This is one of their favourites – I suggested that she add the taurine and bone meal just in case the supply of mice and rodents was low. This dish can be served with a little rice or pasta.

Heat the oil in a heavy pan, and sauté the carrot and onion for a few minutes. Add the lamb cubes and brown on both sides. Stir in the flour and cook gently over a low heat for 1 minute. Gradually stir in the stock to make gravy; cook for a few minutes. Add the bone meal, thyme and taurine. Transfer to a casserole dish and cook at 180°C/350°F/gas-mark 4 for 30 to 40 minutes.

SAUSAGE-AND-OATMEAL MASH

1 butcher's herbal-beef sausage
1 teaspoon grated carrot
1 teaspoon finely chopped greens
1 dessertspoon potato (mashed using
butter and milk)
1 dessertspoon quickly cooked rolled oats
½ teaspoon iodised salt

*Not just any old sausage – you may find that
speciality sausages also appeal to your cat.*

Burmese and Siamese cats can be finicky eaters, according to
Audrey Bradburn of Wales, who, during one particularly bad
period of fussiness, desperately fed her cats just a sausage. It
was an inspired attempt – they greedily ate the lot. Needless
to say, it was not just any old sausage, but a fine blend of meats
and herbs from the local butcher. But what an easy dish!

Prepare the potato and rolled oats; mix together. Plunge
the carrot and greens into boiling water for a minute and
drain. Add to the mixture. Grill the sausage well, cut it
into small pieces and stir into the purée with the salt.

Poultry

Poultry is the most prevalent and useful source of flesh protein. It can be bought in convenient and economical pieces, and there's no point in indulging in the more expensive breasts. You are not doing your cat a favour, because the muscle meats contained in the legs, wings and thighs are healthier for it. Left-over poultry from the family table is easy to recycle into dishes that keep well in the refrigerator.

CAT'S CHICKEN MOULD

1 chicken carcass and/or various left-over bones
3 garlic cloves, crushed
1 onion, quartered
2 carrots, sliced in two
1 stalk celery
1 teaspoon iodised salt
1 teaspoon thyme
1 teaspoon finely chopped parsley

Most households eat chicken in one form or other once a week, and although we may consider the carcass or assorted bits of leg and wing bones to be only good enough for the dustbin, they contain a lot that is of considerable nutritional value to cats. This dish is a constant favourite with my cats. On cooling, it turns into a marvellous jelly, which can be mixed with pasta, rice and canned or dried commercial foods. It is chock-full of protein, vitamins and minerals, and cats also like the texture.

Clean the carcass and bones of all the accessible meat, cutting away any gristle and sinews; break or chop the bones into small pieces – the skin should be very finely chopped. Put aside. Place the carcass, bones, garlic, carrots, celery, salt and thyme into a sturdy pot, cover with water and bring to the boil; turn down the heat and simmer for 1 hour. Strain, but pick out the carrots. Return the clear liquid to the heat and reduce further; add the pieces of chicken and simmer for 5 to 7 minutes. There should not be too much liquid – if there is, pour some off and keep it separately. Take off the heat. Mash up the cooked carrot and stir it into the chicken, together with the fresh parsley. Cool, cover and refrigerate for 2 to 3 hours to allow the jelly to set.

TURKEY OR CHICKEN BURGERS WITH SOURED CREAM OR YOGURT

3 tablespoons minced turkey (or chicken)
1 garlic clove, crushed
1 tablespoon wholemeal breadcrumbs
1 egg, beaten
¼ teaspoon iodised salt
¼ teaspoon thyme
1 teaspoon olive oil
1 teaspoon chopped greens or parsley
1 tablespoon soured cream or natural, Greek-style yogurt

Burgers can be made from minced or finely chopped left-overs, as well as from fresh meat. They cannot be stored, however, but instead need to be served as soon as they have cooled. I find them a very quick fix for a hungry, agitated cat when I'm late getting home.

Mix together the turkey or chicken, garlic, soured cream or yogurt, beaten egg and half the breadcrumbs. Stir in the salt, thyme and chopped greens or parsley. Make into two patties. Coat with the remaining breadcrumbs. Pop in the refrigerator for a minimum of 10 minutes – 20, if your cat can stand the strain. Heat the olive oil in a skillet; over a high heat brown the burgers on both sides, reduce the heat and cook for a further 6 to 8 minutes; just before they are done, pour in a little water to make some juice. Cool and break up before serving.

STUFFED BRAISED DUCK

1 or more pieces of duck
2 cloves garlic, crushed
1 teaspoon thyme
2 teaspoons butter
½ teaspoon iodised salt
1 apple, peeled and quartered
½ cup chicken stock (made from a cube)
Handful of oatmeal stuffing (page 106)

Duck may sometimes be a bit on the rich side for us, but cats absolutely wallow in the fatty fullness and crispness of this succulent fowl – and it's good for them. This dish is a cinch to prepare. The healthy stuffing recipe is the same as for game. My cats have always liked a very crisp skin (me too), and on serving I cut up the meat and crackly skin into pieces that are too big for them to swallow, but small enough to handle – and then mix them in with the stuffing. The dish can be refrigerated or frozen; thaw it and then sauté it in a little butter over a high heat.

Soften the butter and add the garlic, salt and thyme. Spread over the surface of the duck. Cook the apple in a minimal amount of water for 3 to 5 minutes and then mash it. Prepare the stuffing and arrange it under the duck pieces. Place the duck into an oven-proof, foil-lined dish. Pour over just enough stock to keep the duck afloat. Bake at 230°C /450°F/gas-mark 8 for 1¼ hours.

Fish

Fish is thought to be the ultimate in cat's cuisine. Not so: cats love its smell and taste, but it's not a natural source of food for them. Although cats rarely get around to catching fish themselves, they can certainly find many vital nutrients in all the fluvial and oceanic denizens. Fish can be simply baked, steamed or grilled, but over the years I've managed – with a few additions – to adjust our own ideas of good fish dishes to those that cats both like and benefit from. The most successful are those given here.

SALMON BURGERS

4 oz (125 g) canned salmon
½ cup wholegrain breadcrumbs
½ cup rolled oats
1 egg
½ teaspoon finely chopped parsley
2 teaspoons butter

These nourishing fish burgers take hardly any time to make and can be stored in the refrigerator. You can add extra grated greens or carrots – about a teaspoonful. Tuna can be used instead of salmon, but I find that felines enjoy the latter more.

Mash the salmon; stir in the breadcrumbs, oats and parsley. Beat the egg with a little water. Combine together; form into small patties (any extras can be refrigerated) and cook very fast in hot butter, first on one side, then the other. Cool, break up and serve.

STUFFED MACKEREL, HERRING OR TROUT

1 mackerel, herring or trout,
gutted and cleaned
(heads and bones removed)
2 tablespoons well-cooked brown rice
3 tablespoons oatmeal
2 garlic cloves, crushed
1 teaspoon grated Parmesan cheese
1 tablespoon finely chopped parsley
2 teaspoons natural yogurt

Recent research has proved that mackerel, herring and trout are high in omega 3 fatty acids, which are good fats for cats, as well as for humans: they protect against degenerative diseases, particularly those of the circulation. This dish could be a very positive, healthy addition to your cat's diet.

Mix together the rice, 2 tablespoons of the oatmeal, the garlic, cheese, parsley and yogurt. Fill the washed fish with stuffing – the sides can be held together with toothpicks. Coat with the remaining oatmeal; place on a baking tray. Cook in the oven at 130°C/350°F/gas-mark 4 for 15 minutes. Cool and cut into manageable pieces.

HADDOCK KEDGEREE

8 oz (225 g) smoked haddock
½ cup well-cooked brown rice
1 hard-boiled egg
2 tablespoons natural yogurt, preferably
of the Greek variety
1 teaspoon finely chopped parsley

The feline version is sloppier than ours, because after wondering why my cats spurned this dish at first, I added some fish stock to warm it up for another try. That did the trick. It also has a greater proportion of fish to rice.

Gently poach the haddock in water until it flakes easily (about 8 to 10 minutes). Drain, but reserve the liquid. Remove the skin and bones from the fish and break into large flakes. Cut the hard-boiled egg in half and remove the yolk. Chop up the egg whites and crumble the yolks. Put a little butter in a pan and over a low heat mix together the rice, fish, egg whites, yogurt and parsley, stirring for about 2 to 3 minutes. Add the crumbed yolk and any additional fish-cooking water necessary to make a moist dish.

Pasta and rice

The starchy carbohydrate requirement of cats is virtually nil, but these two grains do provide bulk, and can be used as a basis for the necessary flesh proteins. Having lived in Italy on and off for twenty-five years, I can assure you that cats purr over pasta. In Rome, it is a common sight to see a few cats tucking into spaghetti served on brown paper on both quiet and busy streets. They have also acquired the art of managing the long strings like any other Italian. But for non-Italian cats I recommend cutting up all pasta shapes into small pieces.

TUNA-AND-TOMATO PASTA SAUCE

1 teaspoon olive oil
1 clove garlic, crushed
4 tablespoons chopped tomatoes (from a can)
3 tablespoons tuna (from a can, in vegetable oil)
1 tablespoon brewer's yeast
½ teaspoon iodised salt
1 dessertspoon finely chopped parsley

This is a good standby that can be poured over pasta, rice, or even small squares of wholegrain bread. Just before serving, I often stir in a handful of commercial biscuits, as cats like the crunchiness, and grate about a teaspoon of Parmesan cheese over the top of the dish.

Heat the oil in a pan; lightly cook the garlic, but don't let it brown. Add the tomatoes and stir. Lower the heat and simmer for 10 minutes. Break up the tuna with a fork and stir into the tomatoes, together with the iodised salt and brewer's yeast, and cook for a minute; if it looks too solid, thin it with a little water. Take off the heat and add the parsley. The sauce can be refrigerated.

CHICKEN-LIVER RISOTTO

5 or 6 chicken livers (fresh or frozen)
2 good dabs of butter
1 garlic clove, crushed
Pinch of dried sage
¼ teaspoon iodised salt
1 tablespoon brown rice
⅔ cup chicken stock (made from a
bouillon cube)
1 dessertspoon finely chopped parsley or
other greens
1 teaspoon grated carrot
1 teaspoon grated Parmesan cheese

As far as cats are concerned, chicken livers are paw-lickin' good. Fortunately, they are also a great source of protein, vitamins and minerals. However, as a concentrated food they can be too much of a good thing, so in this meal the livers are balanced with some rice and fresh vegetables.

Lightly brown the rice in a dab of butter, then gradually add the chicken stock, stirring now and then so that it is slowly absorbed and the rice swells – well cooked but very moist. This takes about 20 to 30 minutes. At the last minute, stir in the salt. Meanwhile, cut up the chicken livers into small pieces and cook in the other dab of butter together with the garlic, sage and grated vegetables or parsley for about 5 minutes. Combine the rice and livers and stir in the Parmesan cheese.

Cats tucking into spaghetti are
a common sight in Rome.

RISOTTO ALLA PESCATORE

1 lb (500 g) assorted fish
2 cups fish stock (recipe on
page 97)
½ cup brown rice
1 tablespoon butter
½ teaspoon iodised salt
1 tablespoon brewer's yeast
1 tablespoon bone meal
2 cloves garlic, crushed
1 dessertspoon finely
chopped parsley

In other words, rice with any fish that you can find: fresh, left-over, white, oily or shellfish. Of course, your cat could happily eat the fish as it is without the additional rice, but fish goes further this way, and is also appetisingly moist to eat. This dish can be refrigerated and warmed up.

Heat the stock (if not freshly prepared). Put the butter in a heavy pan, stir in the rice, and cook until it is well impregnated with the butter. Add 1 cup of stock, stirring every now and then; when all is absorbed, gradually add the rest. Rice cooks in 20 to 30 minutes. During the final minutes, stir in the salt, brewer's yeast and bone meal. Chop the fish into small pieces, removing all bones. In another pan, heat a little butter and stir in the garlic and parsley; add the fish, tossing it around with a fork. You might need to add some stock if the dish looks too dry. Combine the rice and fish and serve.

This recipe is a perfect example of adapting a family meal for your cat. It will be exceedingly grateful to have this dish placed before it.

Recommended further reading

Juliette de Baïracli Levy,
The complete herbal handbook for the dog and cat,
Faber and Faber, London, UK, and Boston, USA.

Edmund R Dorosz, BSA, DVM,
Let's cook for our cat,
Our Pet's Inc, PO Box 2094,
Fort Macleod, Alberta, Canada.
(Available in the UK by mail from Abbeywood Publishing,
PO Box 1, Longnor, Derbyshire SK17 0JD.)

Dr Bruce Fogle,
The encyclopaedia of the cat,
Dorling Kindersley, London, UK.

Anitra Frazier,
The new natural cat,
Aurum Press (UK) and Dutton (USA).

Ann N Martin,
Food pets die for,
New Sage Press, Oregon, USA.

Richard H Pitcairn, DVM, PHD & Susan Hubble Pitcairn,
Natural health for dogs and cats,
Rodale Press, Emmaus, Pennsylvania, USA.
(Available in the UK by mail from Rodale Health Books,
Marlborough Road, Aldbourne, Marlborough, Wilts SN8 2HP.)

The editors of *Prevention Magazine*,
Home remedies for dogs and cats,
Rodale Press, Emmaus, Pennsylvania, USA.(Available in the UK
by mail from Rodale Health books, Marlborough Road,
Aldbourne, Marlborough, Wilts SN8 2HP.)

Useful addresses

IN THE UK:
British Association of Homeopathic Veterinary Surgeons
Alternative Veterinary Medicine Centre
Chinham House
Stanford-in-the-Vale
Farringdon, Oxon SN7 8NQ

(*Send sae for information about veterinarians using homeopathy and natural therapies for cats.*)

Feline Advisory Bureau
Taeselbury
High Street
Tisbury, Wilts SP3 6LD

IN THE USA:
American Holistic Veterinary Medical Association
2214 Old Emmorton Road
Bel Air
Maryland 21015

(*Members also listed on the web site www.altvetmed.com*)

Index

To my dear freind, Semiramis, who first introduced me to the joy of cats in Rome and on the island of Capri.

First published in Great Britain in 1998
by George Weidenfeld & Nicolson
The Orion Publishing Group Ltd
5 Upper Saint Martin's Lane
London WC2H 9EA
Text copyright © Bronwen Meredith,
1998
Illustrations copyright © Graham
Oakley, 1998
Design and layout copyright ©
Weidenfeld & Nicolson, 1998

Editorial director: Susan Haynes
Art director: David Rowley
Designer: Nigel Soper
Edited by: Clare Haworth-Maden

A CIP catalogue record for this book is
available from the British Library
ISBN 0 297 82415 5
Printed in Italy